ISBN 978-1-332-80816-8
PIBN 10461033

This book is a reproduction of an important historical work. Forgotten Books uses
state-of-the-art technology to digitally reconstruct the work, preserving the original format
whilst repairing imperfections present in the aged copy. In rare cases, an imperfection in
the original, such as a blemish or missing page, may be replicated in our edition. We do,
however, repair the vast majority of imperfections successfully; any imperfections that
remain are intentionally left to preserve the state of such historical works.

1 MONTH OF
FREE
READING

at
www.ForgottenBooks.com

By purchasing this book you are
eligible for one month membership to
ForgottenBooks.com, giving you
unlimited access to our entire
collection of over 700,000 titles via
our web site and mobile apps.

To claim your free month visit:
www.forgottenbooks.com/free461033

English
Français
Deutsche
Italiano
Español
Português

www.forgottenbooks.com

Mythology Photography **Fiction**
Fishing Christianity **Art** Cooking
Essays Buddhism Freemasonry
Medicine **Biology** Music **Ancient**
Egypt Evolution Carpentry Physics
Dance Geology **Mathematics** Fitness
Shakespeare **Folklore** Yoga Marketing
Confidence Immortality Biographies
Poetry **Psychology** Witchcraft
Electronics Chemistry History **Law**
Accounting **Philosophy** Anthropology
Alchemy Drama Quantum Mechanics
Atheism Sexual Health **Ancient History**
Entrepreneurship Languages Sport
Paleontology Needlework Islam
Metaphysics Investment Archaeology
Parenting Statistics Criminology
Motivational

HE RESURRECTION OF JESUS

By

JAMES ORR, M.A., D.D

Professor of Apologetics and Systematic Theology in the United Free Church College, Glasgow

"He is not here; for He is risen, even as He said."

HODDER AND STOUGHTON

LONDON MCMVIII

Butler and Tanner The Selwood Printing Works Frome and London

CONTENTS.

6 CONTENTS

PAGE

VI

CREDIBILITY *continued*—THE POST-RESURRECTION
APPEARANCES.   143

VII

THE SIGNIFICANCE OF THE APPEARANCES—THE RISEN
BODY   173

VIII

THE APOSTOLIC CHURCH—VISIONAL AND APPARITIONAL
THEORIES   205

IX

NEO-BABYLONIAN THEORIES—JEWISH AND APO-
CRYPHAL IDEAS   235

X

DOCTRINAL BEARINGS OF THE RESURRECTION .   .   265

INDEX   289

THE PRESENT STATE OF

THE PRESENT STATE OF THE QUESTION

A RESTATEMENT of the grounds of belief in the great fact of the Lord's Resurrection seems called for in view of the changed forms of assault on this article of the Christian faith in recent years. It is difficult, indeed, to isolate this particular fact, outstanding as it is, from its context in the Gospel history taken as a whole, every point in which is made subject to a like minute and searching criticism. On the other hand, the consideration of the evidence for the Resurrection may furnish a vantage ground for forming a better estimate of the value of the methods by which much of the hostile criticism of the Gospels is at present carried on.

As preliminary to the inquiry, it is desirable that a survey should be taken of the changed lights in which the question appears in past and in contemporary thought.

Time was, not so far removed, when the Resurrection of Jesus was regarded as an immovable corner-stone of Christianity. A scholar and historian like the late Dr. Arnold, of Rugby, summed up a general belief when he wrote · " I have been used for many years to study the history of other times, and to examine and weigh the evidence of those who have written about them ; and I know of no fact in the history of mankind which is proved by better and fuller evidence of every sort, to the understanding of a fair inquirer, than the great sign which God has given us, that Christ died and rose again from the dead." [1] It will be recognized by any one familiar with the signs of the times that this language could not be employed about the state of belief to-day.

It was not that this article of Christian belief had not been long enough and violently enough assailed. The Resurrection of Jesus has been a subject of controversy in all ages. The story which St. Matthew tells us was in circulation among the Jews " until this day " [2]—that the disciples had *stolen* the body of Jesus—was still spread abroad in the days of Justin Martyr.[3] It reappears in that grotesque mediæval concoction, the *Toledoth Jeschu*.[4] Celsus, whom Origen combats, ridicules the Christian belief, and, with modern acuteness, urges the contradictions in the Gospel narratives.[5]

---

[1] Sermon on the Sign of the Prophet Jonas.
[2] Matt. xxviii. 15.　　　　[3] *Dial. with Trypho*, 108.
[4] With some difference, in both the Wagenseil (1681) and the Huldreich (1705) recensions.
[5] Origen, *Against Celsus*, ii. 56–63 ; v. 56, 58.

Deistical writers, as Woolston and Chubb, made the Resurrection a chief object of their attacks.[1] On the Continent, from Reimarus to Strauss, the stream of destructive or evasive[2] criticism was kept up. Strauss must be regarded as the most trenchant and remorseless of the assailants even to the present hour.[3] What escaped his notice in criticism of the narratives is not likely to have much force now. If, therefore, faith in the Resurrection till recently remained unshaken, it was not because the belief was not contested, but because of the confident conviction that the attack all along the line had failed. Other elements in the Gospel tradition might be doubtful, but here, it was supposed, was a rock on which the most timorous might plant his feet without fear. Details in the Resurrection narratives themselves might be, probably were, inaccurate; but the central facts—the empty grave, the message to the women, the appearances to the disciples, sustained as these were by the independent witness of Paul in 1 Corinthians xv. 7, the belief of the whole Apostolic

[1] Replied to by Sherlock, West, Paley, etc.

[2] Several writers in this period advocated the theory that Christ's death was only a case of swoon or suspended animation (thus Paulus, Schleiermacher, Hase, etc.). Strauss may be credited with having given this theory its death-blow. See his *New Life of Jesus* (E.T.), i. pp. 13–33; 408–12.

[3] For the full strength of Strauss's criticism the original *Life of Jesus* (1835) should be consulted.

church—stood secure. This temper of certainty is excellently reflected in the Apologetic textbooks of the most recent period. In these the discussion travels along fixed and familiar lines—theories of imposture, of swoon, of subjective hallucination or visions, of objective but *spiritual* manifestations, all triumphantly refuted, and leaving the way open for the only remaining hypothesis, viz., that the event in dispute actually happened.

It is not suggested that Apologetic, up to this recent point, had failed in its main object, or that its confidence in the soundness of its grounds for belief in the Resurrection was misplaced. It is not implied, even, that the evidence which sufficed then is not adequate to sustain faith now. It may turn out that it is, and that in the *essence* of both attack and defence less is really changed than the modern man supposes. Still even the casual observer cannot fail to perceive that, in important respects, the state of the controversy is very different to-day from what it was, say, fifteen or twenty years ago. Forces which were then only gathering strength, or beginning to make themselves felt, have now come to a head, and the old grounds for belief, and the old answers to objections, are no longer allowed to pass unchallenged. The evidence for the Resurrection may be much what it has been for the last nineteen centuries, but the temper of the age in dealing with that evidence has undeniably altered. The subject is approached from new sides, with new presuppositions, with new critical methods and apparatus, with a wider outlook on the religious history of mankind, and a better understanding, derived from comparative study, of the growth of religious myths; and, in the light of this new knowledge, it is confidently affirmed that the old defences are obsolete, and that it is no longer open to the instructed intelligence—" the modern mind," as it is named—to entertain even the possibility of the bodily Resurrection of Christ from the grave. The believer in this divine fact, accordingly, is anew put on his defence, and must speak to purpose, if he does not wish to see the ground taken away from beneath his feet.

It has already been hinted, and will subsequently become more fully apparent, that the consideration of Christ's Resurrection cannot be dissociated from the view taken of the facts which make up the Gospel history as a whole. This should be frankly acknowledged on both sides at the outset. Christ is not divided. The Gospel story cannot be dealt with piecemeal. The Resurrection brings its powerful attestation to the claims made by Jesus in His earthly Ministry;[1] but the claim to Messiahship and divine Sonship, on the other hand, with all the evidence in the Gospels that supports it, must be taken into account when we

---

[1] Rom. i. 4.

are judging of the reasonableness and probability of the Resurrection. No one can, even if he would, approach this subject without some prepossessions on the character, claims, and religious significance of Jesus, derived from the previous study of the records of His life, or, going deeper, from the presuppositions which have governed even that study. The believer's presupposition is Christ. If Christ was what His Church has hitherto believed Him to be—the divine Son and Saviour of the world—there is no antecedent presumption against His Resurrection; rather it is incredible that He should have remained the prey of death.[1] If a lower estimate is taken of Christ, the historical evidence for the Resurrection will assume a different aspect. It will then remain to be seen which estimate of Christ most entirely fits in with the totality of the facts. On that basis the question may safely be brought to an issue.

This leads to the remark that it is really this question of *the admissibility of the supernatural* in the form of miracle which lies at the bottom of the whole investigation. The repugnance to miracle which is so marked a characteristic of the " modern " criticism of the Gospels can hardly, without an ignoring of the course of discussion for at least the last century and a half, be spoken of as a " new " thing. It underlay the rationalism

[1] Acts ii. 24.

of the older period, and some of the most stinging words in Strauss's *Life of Jesus* are directed against the abortive attempts of well-meaning mediating theologians to evade this fundamental issue. Strauss's own position is made clear beyond possibility of mistake, and anticipates everything the " modern " man has to urge on the subject. " Our modern world," he says, " after many centuries of tedious research, has attained a conviction that all things are linked together by a chain of causes and effects, which suffers no interruption. . . . The totality of things forms a vast circle, which, except that it owes its existence and laws to a superior power, suffers no intrusion from without. This conviction is so much a habit of thought with the modern world, that in actual life the belief in a supernatural manifestation, an immediate divine agency, is at once attributed to ignorance and imposture." [1] Strauss at this stage is persuaded that " the essence of the Christian faith is perfectly independent of his criticism "; that " the supernatural birth of Christ, His miracles, His resurrection and ascension, remain eternal truths, whatever doubts may be cast on their reality as historical facts "; and that " the dogmatic significance of the life of Jesus remains inviolate." [2] At a later period, in his book on *The*

---

[1] The words are from the fourth edition (1840) of the (older) *Life of Jesus* (E.T.) i. p. 71. [2] Ibid. Pref. p. xi.

Old and the New Faith, he reached the true gravi-
tation level of his speculations, and in answer to
the question, " Are we still Christians ? " boldly
answered " No." [1]

The " modern " man has thus no reason to
plume himself on his denial of miracle as a brand-
new product of the scientific temper of the age
in which he lives. His " modernity " goes back
a long way in its negations. What is to be admitted
is that the magnificent advance of the sciences
during the past century has accentuated and
reinforced this temper of distrust (or positive
denial) of the miraculous ; has given it greater
precision and wider diffusion ; has furnished it
with new and plausible reasons, and made it more
formidable as a practical force to be encountered.
There is no doubt, in any case, that this spirit
rules in a large proportion of the works recently
issued on the Gospels and on the life of Christ,
and is the concealed or avowed premiss of their
treatment of the miraculous element in Christ's
history, and notably of His Resurrection.[2] The
same temper has insensibly spread through a large
part of the Christian community. Dr. Sanday

---

[1] In 1872.

[2] One may name almost at random such writers as
A. Sabatier, Harnack, Pfleiderer, Wernle, Weinel, Wrede,
Wellhausen, Schmiedel, Bousset, Neumann, O. Holtzmann,
F. Carpenter, Percy Gardner, G. B. Foster (Chicago),
N. Schmidt, K. Lake, etc.

truly enough describes " the attitude of many a loyal Christian " when he says that " he [the Christian] accepts the narratives of miracles and of the miraculous as they stand, but with a note of interrogation." [1] Others frankly reject them altogether. A chief difficulty in dealing with this widely-spread tendency is that it is, in most cases, less the result of reasoning than, as just said, a " temper," due to what Mr. Balfour would call " a psychological climate," [2] or Lecky would describe as " the general intellectual condition " of the time.[3] Still, it is only by fair reasoning, and the adducing of considerations which set things in a different light, that it can be legitimately met ; apart, that is, from a change in the " climate " itself, a thing continually happening. When this is done, it is remarkable how little, in the end, it is able to say in justification of its sweeping assumptions.

It is not only, however, in the general temper of the time that a change has taken place in the treatment of our subject ; the new spirit has

[1] *The Life of Christ in Recent Research*, p. 103.

[2] " A psychological ' atmosphere ' or ' climate ' favourable to the life of certain modes of belief, unfavourable, and even fatal, to the life of others."—*Foundations of Belief*, fourth edition, p. 218.

[3] See the " Introduction " to Lecky's *History of Rationalism in Europe*, and his interesting summary of the causes of " The Declining Sense of the Miraculous " in the close of chap. ii. of that work.

armed itself with new weapons, and, first of all, with those supplied to it in the methods and results of the *later textual and historical criticism.* Even the tyro cannot be unaware of the almost revolutionary changes wrought in the forms and methods of New Testament criticism—following in the wake of Old Testament criticism [1]—within the last generation. There is, to begin with, an enormous increase in the materials of criticism, with its results in greater specialization and increased urgency in the demand for a many-sided equipment in the textual critic, commentator, and historical writer.[2] Then, with extension of knowledge, has come a sharpening of intelligence and increased stringency of method—a painstakingness in research, an attention to detail, aptitude in seizing points of relation and contrast, skill in disentangling difficulties, fertility in suggestion— above all, a boldness and enterprise in speculation [3]—which leave the older and more cautious scholarship far in the rear. Doubtless, if the Resurrection be truth, the application of these

[1] It is a sign of the times that Old Testament scholars like Wellhausen and Gunkel are now transferring their attentions to the New Testament.

[2] See the remarkable catalogue of qualifications for the commentator set forth in the Preface to Mr. W. C. Allen's new commentary on St. Matthew (*Intern. Crit. Com.*).

[3] Dr. Sanday notes this as a characteristic of recent work on the Gospels. See his *Life of Christ in Recent Research,* p. 41.

stricter methods should only make the truth the more apparent. But it is obvious also that, for those who care to use them in that way, the methods furnish ready aids for the disintegration of the text and evaporation of its historical contents. If a passage for any reason is distasteful, the resources in the critical arsenal are boundless for getting it out of the way. There is slight textual variation, some MS. or version omits or alters, the Evangelists conflict, it is unsuitable to the speaker or the context, if otherwise unchallengeable, it is late and unreliable tradition. Wellhausen's *Introduction to the First Three Gospels* is an illustration of how nearly everything which has hitherto been of interest and value in the Gospels—Sermon on the Mount and parables included—disappears under this kind of treatment.[1] Schmiedel's article on the " Gospels " in the *Encyclopædia Biblica* is a yet more extreme example. The application of the method to our immediate subject is admirably seen in Professor Lake's recent book on *The Historical Evidence for the Resurrection of Jesus Christ*. A painfully minute and unsparing verbal criticism of the Gospel narratives and of the references in Paul results naturally in the conclusion that there is *no* evidence of any value—except, perhaps, for the general fact of " appearances "

[1] See his *Einleitung*, pp. 52–57, 68–72, 86–87, 90–93, etc.

to the disciples. No fibre of the history is left standing as it was. Material assistance is afforded to this type of criticism by the theory of the relations of the Gospels which is at present the prevailing one—what Mr. Allen believes to be " the one solid result of literary criticism," [1] viz., the dependence of the first and third Gospels, in their narrative portions, on the " prior " Gospel of St. Mark. It is temptingly easy, on this theory, to regard everything in these other Gospels which is not found in, or varies from, St. Mark, as a wilful " writing up " or embellishment of the original simpler story ; as something, therefore, to be at once set aside as unhistorical. [2]

These which have been named are dogmatic and literary assaults ; but now, from yet another. side, a formidable attack is seen developing on the historicity of the narratives of the Resurrection—namely, from the side of *comparative religion and mythology*. It is in itself nothing new to draw comparisons between the Resurrection of Jesus and the stories of death and resurrection in pagan religions. Celsus of old made a beginning in this direction. [3] The myths, too, on which

---

[1] *St. Matthew*, Pref. p. vii. It is not to be assumed that this judgment, on which more will be said after, is acquiesced in by every one. Cf. chap. iii.

[2] This is pretty much Wellhausen's method, except that Wellhausen attaches little or no historical value even to St. Mark. Prof. Lake follows in the same track.

[3] Origen, *Against Celsus*, ii. 55–58.

reliance is placed in these comparisons are, in many cases, really there,[1] and frequently collections have been made of them for the purpose of discrediting the Christian belief. The subject may now be said to have entered on its scientific phase in the study of comparative mythology—for instance, in such a work as Dr. J. G. Frazer's *Golden Bough*[2]—and as the result of the long train of discoveries throwing light on the religious beliefs and mythological conceptions of the most ancient peoples—Babylonian, Egyptian, Arabian, Persian, and others. In its newest form—sometimes called the " Pan-Babylonian," though there is yet great diversity of standpoint, and no little division of opinion, among the writers to whom the name is applied—the movement has already attained to imposing proportions, and has given birth to an important literature. Among its best-known representatives on the Continent, of different types, are H. Winckler, A. Jeremias, H. Gunkel, P. Jensen; Dr. Cheyne may speak for it here. A chief characteristic of the school is that, declining to look at any people or religion in isolation from general history, it aims at explaining any given religion from the circumstances of its environ-

---

[1] Myths of death and resurrection are prominent in the ancient Mysteries. This phase of the subject will be discussed after.

[2] Cf. also L. R. Farnell's book, *The Evolution of Religion*.

ment, and from analogies and parallels drawn from other religions. Conceptions dérived ultimately from Babylonia were spread through the whole East, and these, entering through many channels, had a powerful influence in moulding, first the Israelitish, then the Christian religions. Winckler boldly applied his theory to the religious ideas and history of the Old Testament; Gunkel and the others named [1] extend it to the New. "Conservative theologians," writes Dr. Cheyne, "will have to admit that the New Testament now has to be studied from the point of view of mythology as well as from that of philological exegesis and Church-history. . . . For that harmonious combination of points of view which is necessary for the due comprehension of the New Testament, it is essential that the help of mythology, treated of course by strictly critical methods, should be invoked. In short, there are parts of the New Testament—in the Gospels, in the Epistles, and in the Apocalypse—which can only be accounted for by the newly-discovered fact of Oriental syncretism, which began early and continued late. And the leading factor in this is Babylonian." [2]

The story of the Resurrection is naturally one

[1] Cf. Gunkel's *Zum Religionsgeschichtlichen Verständniss des neuen Testaments*. Jeremias is an exception to the general position in so far that, while accepting the analogies, he does not deny the New Testament facts. See his *Babylonisches im N.T.* [2] *Bible Problems*, pp. 18, 19.

of the "legends" on the rise of which the new Babylonian theory is supposed to be able to cast special light, and Dr. Cheyne gratefully accepts its help.[1] Professor Lake regards it as a theory which, while not proved, "one has seriously to reckon with."[2] Even Dr. Cheyne, however, is outdone, and is stirred to active protest, by the astonishing lengths to which the theory is carried by Professor Jensen in his recent massive work, *The Gilgamesh Epic in World Literature*,[3] which literally transforms the Gospel history into a version of the story of that mythical Babylonian hero! It is the saving fact in theories of this kind that they speedily run themselves into excesses which deprive them of influence to right-thinking minds.[4]

Yet another point of view is reached (though it may be combined with the preceding), when the attempt is made to show that *the idea and spiritual virtue* of Christ's Resurrection can be conserved, while the belief in a bodily rising from the tomb is surrendered. This is the tendency which manifests itself especially in a section of the school of theologians denominated Ritschlian. It connects itself naturally with the disposition in this school to seek the ground of faith in an

---

[1] *Bible Problems*, pp. 21, 115 ff.   [2] *Ut supra*, p. 263.
[3] *Das Gilgamesch-Epos in der Weltliteratur*, Bd. I.
[4] The general theory is discussed in Chap. ix.

immediate religious impression—in something verifiable on its own account—and to dissociate faith from doubtful questions of criticism and uncertainties of historical inquiry. Ritschl himself left his relation to the historical fact of the Resurrection in great obscurity. Of those usually reckoned as his followers, some accept and defend the fact,[1] but the greater number sit loose to the idea of a bodily Resurrection, claiming that it cannot be established by historical evidence, and in any case is not an essential element of faith.[2] Most *reject* the bodily rising as inconsistent with an order of nature. The certainty to which the Christian holds fast is that Christ, his Lord, still lives and rules, but this is, as Herrmann would say, a " thought of faith "—a conviction of Christ's abiding life, based on the estimate of His religious worth, and not affected by any view that may be held as to His physical resuscitation. There can be no doubt that the feeling which this line of argument represents is very widely spread.

The name which most readily occurs in connexion with the view of the Resurrection now indicated is that of Professor Harnack, whose Berlin lectures, translated under the title, *What*

---

[1] E.g., Kaftan, Loofs, Häring.

[2] Among those who take this position may be named Herrmann, J. Weiss, Wendt, Lobstein, Reischle, etc. Some of these admit supernatural impressions. See below, chap. viii.

PRESENT STATE OF THE QUESTION 25

is Christianity ? [1] have helped not a little to popu-
larize it. Harnack had earlier unambiguously
stated his position in his *History of Dogma.* " Faith,"
it is there contended, " has by no means to do
with the knowledge of the form in which Jesus
lives, but only with the conviction that He is
the living Lord." " We do not need to have
faith in a fact, and that which requires religious
belief, that is, trust in God, can never be a fact
which would hold good apart from that belief.
The historical question and the question of faith
must, therefore, be clearly distinguished here."
He seeks to show the weakness of the historical
evidence—" even the empty grave on the third
day can by no means be regarded as a certain
historical fact "—and declares · " (1) that every
conception which represents the Resurrection of
Christ as a simple reanimation of His mortal body
[no one affirms that it is] is far from the original
conception, and (2) that the question generally as
to whether Christ has risen can have no existence
for any one who looks at it apart from the contents
and worth of the Person of Jesus." [2] Quite to
the same effect, if in warmer language, Harnack
distinguishes in his Berlin lectures between what
he calls " the Easter message " and " the Easter
faith "—the former telling us of " that wonderful

---

[1] *Das Wesen des Christentums.*
[2] Eng. trans. i. pp. 85–86.

event in Joseph of Arimathæa's garden, which, however, no eye saw"; the latter being "the conviction that the Crucified One still lives; that God is just and powerful; that He who is the firstborn among many brethren still lives." The former, the historical foundation, faith "must abandon altogether, and with it the miraculous appeal to our senses." Nevertheless, "Whatever may have happened at the grave and in the manner of the appearances, one thing is certain · this grave was the birthplace of the indestructible belief that death is vanquished, that there is a life eternal." [1] The logic is not very easy to follow, but this is not the place to criticise it. Enough if it is made clear how this mode of conceiving of the Resurrection of Christ, which imports a · new element into the discussion, presents itself to the minds that hold it.

The "appearances" to the disciples, however, still are there, variously and well attested, as by St. Paul's famous list in 1 Corinthians xv. 4–8, as to which even Strauss says : "There is no occasion to doubt that the Apostle Paul heard this from Peter, James, and perhaps from others concerned (cf. Gal. i. 18 ff., ii. 9), and that all of these, even the five hundred, were firmly convinced that they had seen Jesus who had been dead and was alive again." [2]

---

[1] *What is Christianity ?* E.T., 1900, pp. 161–2.
[2] *New Life of Jesus,* 1. p. 400.

What is the explanation ? Were they simply, as Strauss thought, visions, hallucinations, delusions ? Here is a new dividing-line, even among those who reject the reality of the Lord's bodily Resurrection. The appearances were too real and persistent, they feel, to be explained as the mere work of the imagination. Phantasy has its laws, and it does not operate in this strange way. There were appearances, but may they not have been *appearances of the spiritually risen* Christ, manifestations from the life beyond the grave by one whose body was still sleeping in the tomb ? So thought Keim, who argued powerfully against the subjective visionary theory [1]—so thinks even Professor Lake.[2]

The idea is not wholly a new one,[3] but Keim brought new support to it in his *Jesus of Nazara*, and since then it has commended itself to many minds, who have found in it a *via media* between complete denial of the Resurrection and acceptance of the physical miracle of the bodily rising. It has obtained the adhesion of not a few of the members of the Ritschlian school.[4]

All this belongs to the older stage of the controversy. It perhaps would not have sufficed to bring

[1] *Jesus of Nazara* (E.T.), vi. pp. 323 ff.
[2] *Ut supra*, pp. 271–6.
[3] It appears in Schenkel, Weisse, Schweitzer, and others.
[4] Among these Bornemann, Reischle, and others, leave the question open : J. Weiss argues for supernatural impressions, etc.

about a revival of the theory but for the new turn given to speculation on appearances of the dead by the investigations and reports of the Society of Psychical Research. It is to "the type of phenomena collected" by this Society, "and specially by the late Mr. F. W. H. Myers," that Professor Lake attaches himself in his hypothetical explanation.[1] His position, as stated by himself, is a curious inversion of the older one. Formerly, the Resurrection of Jesus was thought to be a guarantee of the future life—of immortality. Now, it appears, the future life "remains merely a hypothesis until it can be shown that personal life does endure beyond death, is neither extinguished nor suspended, and is capable of manifesting its existence to us."[2] Professor Lake has not the sanguineness of Professor Harnack. He thinks that "some evidence" has been produced by men of high scientific standing connected with the above Society, but "we must wait until the experts have sufficiently sifted the arguments for alternative explanations of the phenomena before they can actually be used as reliable evidence for the survival of personality after death."[3] The belief in the Resurrection of Christ even in the *spiritual* sense—that is, as survival of personality—depends on the success of these same experiments of the Psychical Research Society.

---

[1] *Ut supra*, p. 272.   [2] Ibid. p. 245.   [3] Ibid.

This theory, it will naturally occur, is not a theory of " Resurrection," in the New Testament sense of that word at all ; but we have to do here with the fact that some people believe that it is, or, at least, that it represents the reality which lies behind the narratives of Resurrection in the Gospels. Mr. Myers himself identifies the two things, and, as illustrating this phase of speculation, which has assumed, in an age of unbelief in the supernatural, a semi-scientific aspect, it may be useful, in closing, to quote his own words :—

" I venture now," he says, " on a bold saying for I predict that, in consequence of the new evidence, all reasonable men, a century hence, will believe the Resurrection of Christ, whereas, in default of the new evidence, no reasonable men, a century hence, would have believed it. The ground of the forecast is plain enough. Our ever-growing recognition of the continuity, the uniformity of cosmic law has gradually made of the alleged uniqueness of any incident its almost inevitable refutation.

And especially as to that central claim, of the soul's life manifested after the body's death, it is plain that this can less and less be supported by remote tradition alone ; that it must more and more be tested by modern experience and inquiry. . . . Had the results (in short) of ' psychical research ' been purely negative, would not Christian evidence—I do not say Christian *emotion*, but Christian *evidence*—have received an overwhelming blow ?

" As a matter of fact—or, if you prefer the phrase, in my own personal opinion—our research has led us to results of a quite different type. They have not been negative only, but largely positive. We have shown that, amid much deception and self-deception, fraud and illusion, veritable manifestations do reach us from beyond the grave. The central claim of Christianity is thus confirmed, as never before. . . . There is nothing to hinder the conviction that, though we be all ' the children of the Highest,' He came nearer than we, by some space by us immeasurable, to that which is infinitely far. There is nothing to hinder the devout conviction that He of His own act ' took upon Him the form of a servant,' and was made flesh for our salvation, foreseeing the earthly travail and the eternal crown." [1]

[1] *Human Personality and its Survival*, II., pp. 288–9.

ITS NATURE

ITS NATURE AS MIRACLE

IT is granted on all sides that the Christian Church was founded on, or in connexion with, an energetic preaching of the Lord's Resurrection from the dead. The *fact* may be questioned : the *belief* will be admitted.

" In the faith of the disciples," Baur says, " the Resurrection of Jesus Christ came to be regarded as a solid and unquestionable fact. It was in this fact that Christianity acquired a firm basis for its historical development." [1]

Strauss speaks of " the crowning miracle of the Resurrection—that touchstone, as I may well call it, not of Lives of Jesus only, but of Christianity itself," and allows that it " touches Christianity to the quick," and is " decisive for the whole view of Christianity." [2]

" The Resurrection," says Wellhausen, " was the foundation of the Christian faith, the heavenly Christ, the living and present Head of the disciples." [3]

---

[1] *History of the First Three Centuries* (E. T.) i. p. 42.
[2] *New Life of Jesus*, i. pp. 41, 397.
[3] *Einleitung in die Drei Ersten Evangelien*, p. 96.

" For any one who studies the marvellous story of the rise of the Church," writes Dr. Percy Gardner, " it soon becomes clear that that rise was conditioned—perhaps was made possible—by the conviction that the Founder was not born, like other men, of an earthly father, and that His body did not rest like those of other men in the grave.   " [1]

" The Resurrection of the Lord Jesus Christ," says Canon Henson, " has always been regarded as the corner-stone of the fabric of Christian belief; and it certainly has from the first been offered by the missionaries of Christianity as the supreme demonstration of the truth which in that capacity they are charged to proclaim." [2]

" There is no doubt," affirms Mr. F. C. Burkitt, " that the Church of the Apostles believed in the Resurrection of their Lord." [3]

All which simply re-echoes what the Apostle Paul states of the general belief of the Church of his time. " For I delivered unto you first of all that which also I received: that Christ died for our sins according to the Scriptures; and that He was buried: and that He hath been raised on the third day according to the Scriptures." [4]

Here then, is a conceded point—*the belief of the Apostolic Church in the Resurrection of the Lord.* It

[1] *A Historic View of the New Testament,* Lect. v., Sect. 5.
[2] *The Value of the Bible and Other Sermons,* p. 201.
[3] *The Gospel History and its Transmission,* p. 74.
[4] I Cor. xv. 3, 4.

is well to begin with this point, and to inquire what the *nature* of the belief of the earliest Church was. Was it belief in visionary or spiritualistic appearances ?   Belief in the survival of the *soul* of Jesus ? Belief that somehow or somewhere Jesus lived with God, while His body saw corruption in the tomb ? Or was it belief that Jesus had actually risen in the body from the grave ?   That He had been truly dead, and was as truly alive again ?

If the latter was the case, then beyond all question the belief in the Resurrection of Jesus was belief in a true *miracle*, and there is no getting away from the alternative with which this account of the origin of Christianity confronts us.   Strauss states that alternative for us with his usual frankness   " Here then," he says, " we stand on that decisive point where, in the presence of the accounts of the miraculous Resurrection of Jesus, we either acknowledge the inadmissibility of the natural and historical view of the life of Jesus, and must consequently retract all that precedes, and so give up our whole undertaking, or pledge ourselves to make out the possibility of the result of these accounts, i.e., the origin of the belief in the Resurrection of Jesus, without any corresponding miraculous fact " [1]

Now, that the belief of the Apostles and first disciples was really belief in a *true physical Resurrection* in other words, a Resurrection of the body of Jesus

[1] *Ut supra*, i. p. 397.

from the grave, it seems impossible, in face of the evidence, to doubt. Few of the writers above .cited *do* doubt it, whatever view they may take of the reality lying behind the belief. We are happily not here dependent on the results of a minute criticism of the Gospels or of other New Testament texts. We are dealing with a belief which interweaves itself, directly or indirectly, with the whole body of teaching in the New Testament. If Harnack makes a distinction between the Easter " message " and the Easter " faith," it is certain that the first Christians made no such distinction. This admits of ample proof.

Take first the narratives in the Synoptics. There are three of these, in St. Matthew, St. Mark, and St. Luke, and the cardinal feature in each is the empty tomb, and the message to the women, and through them to the disciples, that the Lord had risen. " He is not here, He is risen." [1] The body had left the sepulchre. It is not otherwise in St. John. The Magdalene, and after her Peter and John, whom she brings to the spot, find the tomb empty.[2] It is to be remembered that there are several other miracles of resurrection in the Gospels,[3] and these

[1] Matt. xxviii. 6 ; Mark xvi. 6 ; Luke xxiv. 6, 22, 24.
[2] John xx. 2–13.
[3] Matt. ix. 18, 23–25 ; Mark v. 33–43 ; Luke vii. 11–15, viii. 49–56 ; John xi. ; cf. Matt. xi. 5, and Christ's repudiation of the Sadducean denial of the resurrection, Matt. xxii. 29–32.

throw light on what was understood by Resurrection in the case of the Master. They were all bodily resurrections. The professed fear of the authorities that the disciples might steal away the body of Jesus, and say, "He is risen from the dead," points in the same direction.[1]

With this belief in the bodily Resurrection correspond the narratives of the appearance of the Risen One to His disciples. It is not the truth of the narratives that is being discussed at this stage, though indirectly that is involved, but the nature of their testimony to the Apostolic belief, and on this point their witness can leave little doubt upon the mind. The appearances to the women,[2] to the Apostles,[3] to the two disciples on the road to Emmaus,[4] to the disciples in Galilee,[5] all speak to a person who has risen in the body—not to an incorporeal spirit or phantom. The conditions of existence of the body were, indeed, in some respects supernaturally altered,[6] as befitted the new state on which it had entered, and was yet more fully to enter. But it was still a body which could be seen, touched, handled; which evinced its identity with the body that had been crucified, by the print of the nails

---

[1] Matt. xxvii. 64.
[2] Matt. xxviii. 9, 10 ; John xx. 14–18 ; cf. Mark xvi. 9.
[3] Luke xxiv. 36–43 ; John xx. 19–29 ; cf. Mark xvi. 14.
[4] Luke xxiv. 13–32.
[5] Matt. xxviii. 16 and 17 ; John xxi.
[6] This is touched on below, pp. 53–4 ; cf. chap. vii.

and the spear-mark in the side.[1]   These marks of
His passion, it is implied, Jesus bears with Him even
in the body of his glory.[2]   He walked with His
disciples, conversed with them, ate with them :
" shewed Himself alive," as Luke says, " after His
passion by many proofs."[3]   If any tangible evidence could be afforded of the real Resurrection
of the Lord from the grave, it was surely furnished
in that wonderful period of intercourse with His
disciples, prior to the final Ascension to His
Father.

What the Gospels attest as the belief of the Apostolic Church on the nature of the Resurrection is
amply corroborated by the witness of St. Paul.   It is,
indeed, frequently argued that since St. Paul, in the
words, " He appeared (ὤφθη) to me also," puts the
appearance of the Lord to himself at his conversion
in the same category with the appearances to the
disciples after the Resurrection,[4] he must have regarded these as, like his own, visionary.[5]   Canon
Henson repeats this objection.   " The Apostle, in

[1] Luke xxiv. 39–40 ; John xx. 24–28.
[2] Cf. Rev. v. and vi.   [3] Acts i. 3.
[4] I Cor. xv. 3–9.
[5] Thus, e.g., Weizsäcker (*Apostolic Age*, E. T. i. pp. 8, 9),
Pfleiderer (*Christian Origins*, E. T., pp. 136–137, 160–161).
Weizsäcker says : " There is absolutely no proof that Paul
presupposed a physical Christophany in the case of the
older Apostles.   Had he done so he could not have put
his own experience on a level with theirs.   But since he
does so we must conclude that he looked upon the visions
of his predecessors in the same light as his own."

classing his own 'vision' of the risen Saviour on the road to Damascus with the other Christophanies, allows us to conclude that in all the appearances there was nothing of the nature of a resuscitated body, which could be touched, held, handled, and could certify its frankly physical character by eating and drinking."[1] This, however, is to miss the very point of the Apostle's enumeration. St. Paul's object in his use of " appeared " is not to suggest that the earlier appearances were visionary, but conversely to imply that the appearance vouchsafed to himself on the road to Damascus was as real as those granted to the others. He, too, had veritably " seen Jesus our Lord."[2] That St. Paul conceived of the Resurrection as an actual reanimation and coming forth of Christ's body from the tomb follows, not only from his introduction of the clause, " and that He was buried,"[3] but from the whole argument of the chapter in Corinthians, and from numerous statements elsewhere in his Epistles.

In 1 Corinthians xv. St. Paul is rebutting the contention of the adversaries in that Church that there is no resurrection from the dead for believers, and he does this by appealing to the Resurrection of Christ. The latter fact does not seem to have been disputed. If there is no resurrection from the dead, St. Paul argues, then Christ has not risen ; if Christ has risen, His Resurrection is a pledge of that of

[1] *Ut supra*, p. 204.   [2] 1 Cor. ix. 1.   [3] 1 Cor. xv. 4.

His people.[1]   It is perfectly certain that the sceptics of Corinth were not denying a merely *spiritual* resurrection ; they evidently believed that death was the extinction of the individual life.[2]   As little is St. Paul contending in his reply for a merely spiritual resurrection.   He contends for a resurrection of the *body*, though in a transformed and spiritualized condition.[3]   Professor Lake will concede as much as this.   " There can be clearly no doubt," he says, " that he [Paul] believed in the complete personal identity of that which rose with that which had died and been buried."[4]   As respects Christ, " He believed that at the Resurrection of Jesus His body was changed from one of flesh and blood to one which was spiritual, incorruptible, and immortal, in such a way that there was no trace left of the corruptible body of flesh and blood which had been laid in the grave."[5]   This, however, need not imply, as Professor Lake supposes it to do,[6] that the transformation was effected all at once, nor exclude such appearances as the Gospels record between the Resurrection and Ascension.

---

[1] 1 Cor. xv. 12–23.   [2] xv. 32.   [3] xv. 33–57.
[4] *Historical Evidence for the Resurrection of Jesus Christ*, p. 20.
[5] Ibid. p. 23.
[6] Ibid. pp. 27 and 35.   Canon Henson argues in the *Hibbert Journal*, 1903–4, pp. 476–93, that there is a contradiction between St. Paul and St. Luke in their conceptions of Christ's Resurrection body.   Cf. below, p. 182.

The Apostle's view of the bodily Resurrection of Jesus is unambiguously implied in the various statements of his other Epistles. Thus, in Romans viii. 11 we have the declaration : " But if the Spirit of Him that raised up Jesus from the dead dwelleth in you, He that raised up Christ Jesus from the dead shall give life also to your mortal bodies through His Spirit that dwelleth in you." Here plainly it is the " mortal body " which is the subject of the quickening. Later, in verse 23 of the same chapter, we have · " Waiting for our adoption, to wit, the redemption of our body." In Ephesians i. 19, 20, " the exceeding greatness of [God's] power to usward who believe," is measured by " that working of the strength of His might which He wrought in Christ, when He raised Him from the dead." In Philippians iii. 10, 11, 21, the hope held out is that the Lord Jesus Christ, awaited from heaven, " shall fashion anew the body of our humiliation that it may be conformed to the body of His glory." The like implication of a bodily Resurrection is found in 1 Thessalonians iv. 13-17, and many more passages.

It seems unnecessary to accumulate evidence to the same effect from the remaining New Testament writings. No one will dispute that this is the conception in St. Peter's address in Acts ii. 24–32, and the statements in 1 Peter i. 3, 21, iii. 21, are hardly less explicit. The Apocalypse emphasizes the fact that Jesus is " the firstborn of the

dead." [1] " I am the first and the last, and the
Living One; and I was dead, and behold, I am
alive for evermore." [2] " These things saith the first
and the last, who was dead, and lived again." [2]

On a fair view of the evidence, therefore, it seems
plain that the belief of the Apostolic Church was
belief in a true bodily Resurrection of Jesus Christ,
and it is as little open to doubt that, if such an event
took place, it was a *miracle*, i.e., a true supernatural
intervention of God, in the strictest sense of the
word. Whether that of itself suffices to debar the
" modern " mind from accepting the Resurrection
as an historical fact is matter for discussion, but
there should be no hesitation in conceding that
a question of miracle is involved.

The only possible alternative to this is to assume
that Jesus at His burial was *not really dead*—that
His supposed death from crucifixion was in reality
a " swoon," and that, having revived in the " cool
air " of the tomb, and issued forth, He was believed
by His disciples to have been raised from the dead.
This naturalistic explanation, although numbering
among its supporters no less great a name than
Schleiermacher's,[4] is now hopelessly discredited. It

---

[1] Rev. i. 5.   [2] i. 17, 18.   [3] ii. 8.

[4] It is doubtful how far Schleiermacher himself remained
satisfied with this explanation given in his *Leben Jesu*
(posthumously published). In his *Der christliche Glaube*
(sect. 99), he takes up a more positive attitude, allowing,
if not a direct, still a mediate connexion with the doctrine

was previously mentioned that Strauss practically gave the swoon theory its death-blow, and little has been heard of it since his time " It is evident," Strauss well says, " that this view of the Resurrection of Jesus, apart from the difficulties in which it is involved, does not even solve the problem which is here under consideration—the origin, that is, of the Christian Church by faith in the miraculous Resurrection of a Messiah. It is impossible that a being who had stolen half-dead out of the sepulchre, who crept about weak and ill, wanting medical treatment, who required bandaging, strengthening, and indulgence, and who still at last yielded to His sufferings, could have given to the disciples the impression that He was a Conqueror over death and the grave, the Prince of Life, an impression which lay at the bottom of their future ministry." [1] The hypothesis, in fact, cannot help passing over into one of fraud, for, while proclaiming Jesus as the Risen Lord, who had ascended to heavenly glory, the Apostles must have known the real state of the case, and have closely kept the secret that their Master was in concealment or had died.

Miracle, therefore, in the Resurrection of Jesus cannot be escaped from, and it is well that this, the most fundamental objection to belief in the

of Christ's Person, inasmuch as anything that reflects on the Apostles reflects back on Christ who chose them.

[1] *Ut supra*, i. p. 412.

Resurrection, should be grappled with at once. It is, as before said, not the Resurrection alone that is involved in this objection, but the whole picture of Christ in the Gospels. That picture, as critics are coming to admit, is the picture of a supernatural Personage throughout.[1] It is at least something to have it recognized that the Resurrection does not stand as an isolated fact, but is congruous with the rest of the Gospel history.

It is, however, precisely this element of the miraculous which, it is boldly declared, the " modern " mind cannot admit. The scientific doctrine of " the uniformity of nature " stands in the way. Nature, it is contended, subsists in an unbroken connexion of causes and effects, determined by immutable laws, and the admission of a breach in • this predetermined order, even in a single instance, would be the subversion of the postulate on which the whole of science rests. For the scientific man to admit the possibility of miracles would be to involve himself in intellectual confusion. Apart, therefore, from the difficulty of proof, which, in face of our experience of the regularity of nature, and of the notorious fallibility of human testimony to

---

[1] Cf. Bousset, *Was wissen wir von Jesus ?* pp. 54, 57. " Even the oldest Gospel," this writer says, " is written from the standpoint of faith ; already for Mark, Jesus is not only the Messiah of the Jewish people, but the miraculous eternal son of God, whose glory shone in this world."

extraordinary events,[1] is held to present another insuperable obstacle to the acceptance of miracle, the very idea of a miraculous occurrence is thought to be precluded. Even Dr. Sanday writes in his latest work, *The Life of Christ in Recent Research* : " We are modern men, and we cannot divest ourselves of our modernity. . . . I would not ask any one to divest himself of those ideas which we all naturally bring with us—I mean our ideas as to the uniformity of the ordinary course of nature." [2] As an illustration from a different quarter, a sentence or two may be quoted from the biographer of St. Francis of Assisi, P. Sabatier, who expresses the feeling entertained by some in as concise a way as any. " If by miracle," he says, " we understand either the suspension or subversion of the laws of nature, or the intervention of the First Cause in certain particular cases, I could not concede it. In this negation physical and logical reasons are secondary ; the true reason—let no one be surprised —is entirely religious ; the miracle is immoral. The equality of all before God is one of the postulates of the religious consciousness, and the miracle, that good pleasure of God, only degrades Him to the level of the capricious tyrants of the earth." [3]

[1] Hume's famous argument against miracles turns in substance on the contrast between our unalterable experience of nature and the fallibility of human testimony to wonderful events.

[2] P. 204.   [3] *Life of St. Francis*, p. 433.

The application of this axiom to the life of Christ in the Gospels, and specially to such a fact as the Resurrection, naturally lays the history, as we possess it, in ruins.[1] There is no need, really, for investigation of evidence ; the question is decided before the evidence is looked at. Professor Lake quotes from Dr. Rashdall with reference to the reanimation or sudden transformation of a really dead body, in " violation of the best ascertained laws of physics, chemistry, and physiology " : " Were the testimony fifty times stronger than it is, any hypothesis would be more possible than that." [2]

A word may here be said on the mediating attempts which have frequently been made, and still are made, to bridge the gulf between this modern view of the uniformity of nature and the older conception of the supernatural as direct interference of God with the order of nature, through the hypothesis of " unknown laws." This is what Dr. Sanday in the above-mentioned work calls " making both ends meet," [3] and it commends itself to him and to others as a possible means

---

[1] Cf., on the other hand, Kaftan's vigorous protest against this modern view of the world in his pamphlet *Jesus und Paulus*, pp. 4, 5, 9, 72. " I am no lover," he says, " of the modern view of the world ; rather I find it astonishing that so many thinking men should be led astray by this bugbear " (*Popanz*).

[2] *Ut supra*, p. 267.   [3] P. 203.

of reconciliation between miracle and science. The hypothesis has its legitimate place in a general philosophy of miracles; for it is certainly not an essential part of the Biblical idea of miracle that natural forces should not be utilized. Even assuming that miracle were confined to the wielding, directing, modifying, combining or otherwise using, the forces inherent in nature, it is impossible to say how much, in the hands of an omniscient, omnipotent Being, this might cover. Still, when all this has been admitted, the real difficulty is not removed. There is a class of miracles in the Gospel—the Virgin Birth and the Resurrection may safely be placed among them, though they are not the only examples—which is not amenable to this species of treatment; miracles which, if accepted at all, unquestionably imply direct action of the Creative Cause. We have no reason whatever to believe—the Society of Psychical Research does not help us here—that hitherto unknown laws or secret forces of nature will ever prove adequate to the instantaneous healing of a leper, or the restoring of life to the dead. It is with regard to this class of miracles that the scientist takes up his ground. Assume what you will, he will say, of wonderful and inexplicable facts due to unknown natural causes: what cannot be admitted is the occurrence of events due to direct Divine intervention; what Hume would speak of as the effects of " particular volitions," [1] or Renan, of " private volitions." [2] These, in his judgment, are cases of the interpolation into nature of a force which breaks through, rends, disrupts, the natural sequence, and can hardly be conceived of otherwise than as a disturbance of the total system. It is this objection the believer in the miracle of the Resurrection has to meet.

. But can it not be met ?   It is granted, of course, that there are views of the universe which exclude miracle absolutely. The atheist, the Spinozist, the materialist, the monist like Haeckel, the abso-lutist, to whom the universe is the logical unfolding of an eternal Idea—all systems, in short, which exclude a Living Personal God as the Author and Upholder of the world—have no alternative but to deny miracle. Miracle on such a conception of the world is rightly called impossible. But that, we must hold, is not the true conception of the relation of God to His world, and the question is not—Is miracle possible on an atheistic, or material-istic, or pantheistic conception of the world ? but, Is it possible and credible on a theistic view—on the view of God as at once immanent in the world, yet subsisting in His transcendent and eternally

[1] *Natural Religion*, Pt. XI.
[2] *Philosophical Dialogues*, E. T., pp. 6 ff.   " Two things appear to me quite certain . . . we find no trace of the action of definite beings higher than man, acting, as Mal-branche says, by private volitions."

complete life above it—All-Powerful, All-Wise, All-Holy, All-Good? It is here, e.g., that a writer like Professor G. B. Foster, in his *Finality of the Christian Religion*, seems utterly inconsistent with himself in his uncompromising polemic against miracles.[1] He would be consistent if he took up Spinoza's position of the identity of God with nature. But he claims to hold by the Father-God of Jesus Christ, and expressly finds fault with "naturalism" because it denies ends, purposes, ruling ideas, the providence of a just and holy God. But by what right, on such a basis, is the supernatural ruled out of the history of revelation, and especially out of the history of Christ? Once postulate a God who, as said, has a being above the world as well as in it, a Being of fatherly love, free, self-determined, purposeful, who has moral aims, and overrules causes and events for their realization, and it is hard to see why, for high ends of revelation and redemption, a supernatural economy should not be engrafted on the natural, achieving ends which could not be naturally attained, and why the evidence for such an economy should on *a priori* grounds be ruled out of consideration. To speak of miracle, with P. Sabatier, from the religious point of view, as "immoral," is simply absurd.

[1] He goes so far as to say that "an intelligent man who now affirms his faith in such stories as actual facts can hardly know what *intellectual* honesty means" (p. 132).

R.J.

4

On such a genuinely theistic conception of the
relation of God to the world and to man, the scientific
objection to miracle drawn from "the uniformity
of Nature," while plausible as an abstract statement, is seen, on deeper probing, to have really very
little force. Professor Huxley and J. S. Mill are
probably as good authorities on science as most,
and both tell us that there is no scientific impossi-
bility in miracle—it is purely and solely a question
of evidence.[1] What, in the first place, is a "law
of nature"? Simply our registered observation
of the order in which we find causes and effects
ordinarily linked together. That they are so linked
together no one disputes. To quote Mr. W. C. D.
Whetham, in his interesting book on *The Recent
Developments of Physical Science*: "Many brave
things have been written, and many capital letters
expended, in describing the Reign of Law. The
laws of Nature, however, when the mode of their
discovery is analyzed, are seen to be merely the
most convenient way of stating the results of experience in a form suitable for future reference.
We thus look on natural laws merely as convenient shorthand statements of the organized
information that at present is at our disposal."[2]
Next, what do we mean by "uniformity" in this

---

[1] Huxley, *Controverted Questions*, pp. 258, 269; Mill,
Logic, Bk. III. chap. xxv.
[2] Pp. 31, 37.

connexion ? Simply that, given like causes opera-
ting under like conditions, like effects will follow.
No one denies this either. Every one will concede
to Dr. Sanday " the uniformity of the *ordinary*
course of nature." If it were otherwise, we should
have no world in which we could live at all. The
question is not, Do natural causes operate uni-
formly ? but, Are natural causes the only causes
that exist or operate ? For miracle, as has frequently been pointed out, is precisely the assertion
of the interposition of a *new* cause ; one, besides,
which the theist must admit to be a *vera causa*.[1]

Not to dwell unduly on these considerations, it
need only further be remarked that it misrepresents
the nature of such a miracle as the Resurrection
of Christ—or of the Gospel miracles generally—to
speak of miracles, with Dr. Rashdall, as " completely isolated exceptions to the laws of nature," [2]
or as arbitrary, capricious breaks in the natural
order, " violations " of nature's laws. Miracles
may well be parts of a system, and belong to a higher
order of causation—though not necessarily a mechani-
cal one. Professor A. B. Bruce, in this connexion,
refers to Bushnell's view of miracles as " wrought
in accordance with a purpose," what he calls " the
law of one's end," and to the phrase used by Bishop
Butler for the same purpose, " general laws of

---

[1] Thus J. S. Mill   [2] See Lake, *ut supra*, p. 268.

wisdom."[1] And is it not the case that, in any worthy theistic view, God must be regarded as Himself the ultimate law of all connexion of phenomena in the universe, and the immanent cause of its changes? This means that a free, holy Will is the ultimate fact to be reckoned with in the interpretation of nature. The ultimate Cause of things has certainly not so bound Himself by secondary laws that He cannot act at will beyond, or in transcendence of them.[2]

The following may be quoted from Professor A. T. Ormond's *Concepts of Philosophy*, as one of the latest utterances from the side of philosophy. Professor Ormond says : " As to the miracle, in any case where it is real, it is either intended in the divine purpose, or it is not. If not, then it has no religious significance. If, however, it be intended in the divine purpose, it then has a place in the world-scheme which evolution itself is working out.

---

[1] *The Miraculous Element in the Gospels*, pp. 65–6 ; cf. Bushnell, *Nature and the Supernatural*, pp. 264–9 ; Butler, *Analogy*, Pt. II. chap. iv. sect. 3.

[2] There are at least three cases in which direct creative action seems to be no " violation " of natural order, but rather to be called for in the interests of that order : (*a*) In the initial act of creation *establishing* the order ; (*b*) in the founding of a *higher* order or kingdom in nature, e.g at the introduction of life (organic nature), (*c*) where the exercise of creative energy is *remedial* or redemptive. In this last case the creative act is not disturbance or destruction of nature, but the restoration of an order already disturbed (Christ's miracles of healing, etc.).

How could a genuine miracle contradict evolution unless we conceive evolution as being absolute? It is not evolution but the form of naturalism we have been criticising, that is inconsistent with any genuine divine happenings." [1]

It is granted, then, that, in the Resurrection of Jesus Christ from the dead, we are in presence of a miracle—a miracle, however, congruous with the character, personal dignity, and claims of Him whose triumph over death is asserted—and there is no evading the issue with which this confronts us, of an actual, miraculous economy of revelation in history. This assuredly was no exception—a single hole drilled in the ordinary uniform course of nature, without antecedents in what had gone before, and consequents in what was to follow. It belongs to a divine system in which miracles must be conceived as interwoven from the beginning. The Resurrection was a demonstration of God's mighty power (" the strength of His might " [2]) ; but was an act in which the Son Himself shared, re-taking to Himself the life He had voluntarily laid down. It is in the light of this miraculous character of the Resurrection we have to consider the phenomena of the appearances of the risen Lord, which otherwise may seem to present features difficult to reconcile. It is an error of Harnack's

[1] *Op. cit.* p. 603.
[2] Eph. i. 19.

to speak of the ordinary conception of the Resurrection as that of " a simple reanimation of His
mortal body." [1] No one will think of it in that
light who studies the narratives of the Gospels.
They show that while Jesus was truly risen in the
body, He had entered; even bodily, on a new phase
of existence, in which some at least of the ordinary
natural limitations of body were transcended.[2]
The discussion of these, however, belongs properly
to another stage, and may here be deferred. Enough
that the central fact be held fast that Jesus truly
manifested Himself in the body in which He was
crucified as Victor over death.

---

[1] *History of Dogma*, E. T. 1. pp. 85–6.

[2] Cf. the remarks on this subject in Dr. Forrest's *The
Christ of History and Experience*, pp. 146 ff., and in Milligan, *The Resurrection of Our Lord*, pp. 12 fl. Dr. Forrest
says · " These contradictory aspects, instead of casting a
suspicion on the appearances, are of the essence of the
problem which they were intended to solve. Christ
hovers, as it were, on the border-line of two different
worlds, and partakes of the characteristics of both, just
because He is revealing the one to the other. . During
the forty days His body was in a transition state, and
had to undergo a further transformation in entering into
the spiritual sphere, its true home " (pp. 150, 152). Pre-
ludings of these changes are seen in the Transfiguration,
the Walking on the Sea, etc.

THE GOSPEL NARRATIVES AND
CAL SOLVENTS

III

THE GOSPEL NARRATIVES AND CRITICAL
SOLVENTS

IT was before stated that a change in the treatment
of the evidence for the Resurrection is necessitated
by the new and more stringent methods of criticism
applied to the narratives of the Gospels, and especially by the theory, now the prevalent one, of the
dependence of the first and third Gospels, in their
narrative parts, on the second—that of St. Mark.
It is desirable, before proceeding further, to give
attention to these new critical methods and their
results, in their bearings on the subject in hand.
It is, of course, too much to ask, even if one had
the competency for the task, that a full discussion
of the Synoptical problem should precede all examination of the narratives of the Resurrection, or that
the Johannine question should be exhaustively
handled before one is entitled to adduce a testimony
from the Fourth Gospel. On the other hand, it
seems imperative that something should be said
on the critical aspect of the subject—enough at
least to indicate the writer's own position, and some

THE GOSPEL NARRATIVES

always with a strict eye on the special point under
investigation.

It will prepare the way for this critical inquiry
if a glance be taken first at the range of the New
Testament material here falling to be dealt with.
The narratives of the Resurrection go together with
the narratives of the burial and of the post-Resurrection appearances of Jesus, and form an inseparable
whole with them. Supplementary to the Gospel
narratives are certain passages in the Book of Acts
and in Paul.

The distribution of the subject-matter may be
thus exhibited :

St. Matthew : Burial, xxvii. 57–66 ; Resurrection,
xxviii. 1–8 ; Appearances, xxviii. 9–20.

St. Mark : Burial, xv. 42–47 ; Resurrection.
xvi. 1–8. *App. to St. Mark :* Appearances, xvi. 9–20.

St. Luke : Burial, xxiii. 50–56 ; Resurrection,
xxiv. 1–12 ; cf. vers. 22–24 ; Appearances, xxiv.
12–53.

St. John : Burial, xix. 38–42 ; Resurrection,
xx. 1–13 ; Appearances, xx. 14–29 ; xxi.

Acts : Appearances, i. 3–11.

St. Paul : Burial and Resurrection, 1 Cor. xv. 4 ;
Appearances, 1 Cor. xv. 5–8.

The narratives thus tabulated contain the historical witness to the Lord's Resurrection, so far
as that witness has been preserved to us. On them,

accordingly, the whole force of critical enginery has been directed, with the aim of discrediting their testimony. The narratives are held to be put out of court (1) On the ground of their manifest discrepancies; (2) Through the application of critical methods to the text; (3) Through the presence of legendary elements in their accounts.

The consideration of the alleged discrepancies can stand over, save as they prove to be involved in the general discussion. Even if all are admitted, they hardly touch the *main* facts of the combined witness—especially the testimony to the central fact of the empty tomb and the Lord's Resurrection on the third day. " No difficulty of weaving the separate incidents," says Dr. Sanday, " into an orderly and well-compacted narrative can impugn the unanimous belief of the Church which lies behind them, that the Lord Jesus rose from the dead on the third day and appeared to the disciples." [1] " There are many variations and discrepancies," writes Mr. F. C. Burkitt, " but all the Gospels agree in the main facts." [2] Strauss' statement of these discrepancies, which he discovers in every particular of the accounts, still remains the fullest and best, and the use he makes of them is not one to the liking of the newer criticism. " Hence," he says, " nothing

---

[1] *Outlines of the Life of Christ*, p. 180 : cf. Alford, *Greek Testament*, i. Prol. p. 20.

[2] *The Gospel History and its Transmission*, p. 223.

but wilful blindness can prevent the perception that no one of the narrators knew and presupposed what another records." [1]

As previously indicated, the critical attack on the narratives of the Resurrection connects itself with the criticism of the Gospels as a whole. The newer criticism is principally distinguished from the older by a different attitude of mind to the Gospel material, and it proceeds by bolder and more assumptive methods. It starts rightly with a painstaking and exhaustive induction of the phenomena to be interpreted; [2] its peculiarity comes to light in the more daring, and often extremely arbitrary way in which it goes about the interpretation. It is no longer held to be enough to determine and explain a text. The newer criticism must get behind the text and show its genesis; must show by comparison with related texts its probable " genealogy; " [3] must take it to pieces, and discover what motive or tendency is at work in it, how it is coloured by environment and modified by later conditions—in brief, how it " grew ": this generally with the assumption that the saying or fact must originally have been something very different from what the text

---

[1] *Life of Jesus*, iii. p. 344.
[2] Illustrations are furnished in the analysis of the linguistic phenomena of the Gospels in Sir John Hawkins' *Horae Synopticae*, Plummer's *St. Luke*, Introd., Harnack's *Lukas der Arzt* (St. Luke and Acts), etc.
[3] Cf. Lake, *Res. of Jesus Christ*, pp. 167–8.

represents it to be. Such a method, no doubt, may open the way to brilliant discoveries, but it may also, and this more frequently, lead to the criticism losing itself in fanciful conjectures. Abundant illustration will be afforded when we come to the examination of the Resurrection narratives.

One question of no small importance is that of the relation of the Synoptical Gospels to each other. It has already been pointed out that the current theory on this subject—what Mr. W. C. Allen and Mr. Burkitt regard as " the one solid result " of the literary criticism of the Gospels—is that St. Matthew and St. Luke, as respects their narrative parts,[1] are based on St. Mark.[2] It is desirable to keep this question in its right place. It would manifestly be a suicidal procedure to base the defence of the Resurrection on the acceptance or rejection of any given solution of the Synoptical problem, especially on the challenge of a theory which has obtained the assent of so many distinguished scholars. Assume it to be finally proved

[1] The supposed *Logia* source does not come into consideration here.

[2] Allen, *St. Matthew*, Pref. p. vii. : " Assuming what I believe to be the one solid result of literary criticism, viz. the priority of the second Gospel to the other two synoptic Gospels." Burkitt, *The Gospel History*, p. 37 : " the one solid contribution," etc. " We are bound to conclude that Mark contains the whole of a document which Matthew and Luke have independently used, and, further, that Mark contains very little besides."

that St. Matthew and St. Luke used St. Mark as
a chief " source," the limits of the evidence for the
Resurrection would be sensibly narrowed, but its
intrinsic force would not be greatly weakened.
St. Mark, after all, is not inventing. He is embodying in his Gospel the common Apostolic tradition
of his time—a tradition which goes back to the
Apostles themselves, and rests on their combined
witness. There is no reason for believing that St.
Mark took the liberties with the tradition, in alter-
ing and " doctoring " it, which some learned
writers suppose. If the other Evangelists, whose
Gospels, on any showing, are closely related to St.
Mark's, adopted the latter as one of their sources,
it can only be because they recognized in that
Gospel a form of the genuine tradition. Their
adoption of it, and working of it up with their own
materials, but set an additional imprimatur on its
contents. At the same time, it is not to be gainsaid that, in practice, the attack on the credit of
the Gospels has been greatly aided by the preva-
lence of this theory of the dependence of the other
Synoptics on St. Mark. As before indicated, it
affords leverage for treating the narratives of the
first and third Gospels as a simple " writing up "
and embellishing of St. Mark's stories, and for rejecting any details not found in the latter as unhistorical and legendary. The *modus operandi* is
expounded by Professor Lake. " When, therefore,"

he says, " we find a narrative which is given in all three Gospels, we have no right to say that we have three separate accounts of the same incident; but we must take the account in Mark as presumably the basis of the other two, and ask whether their variations cannot be explained as due to obscurities or ambiguities in their sources, which they tried to clear up. .   Since Matthew and Luke, so far as they are dealing with the Marcan source, are not first-hand evidence, but rather the two earliest attempts to comment on and explain Mark, we are by no means bound to follow the explanations given by either." [1]

This leads to the question—Is the theory true? Despite its existing prestige, this may be gravely questioned. Detailed discussion would be out of place, but the bearing of the theory on the Resurrection narratives—which will be found to afford some of the most striking disproofs of it—is so direct, that a little attention must be given to it.

The grounds on which the Marcan theory rests are stated with admirable succinctness by Mr. Burkitt. " In the parts common to Mark, Matthew and Luke," he says, " there is a good deal in which all verbally agree; there is also much common to Mark and Matthew, and much common to Mark and Luke, but hardly anything common to Matthew and Luke which Mark does not share also. There

[1] *Ut supra*, p. 45.

is very little of Mark which is not more or less adequately represented either in Matthew or in Luke. Moreover, the common order is Mark's order. Matthew and Luke never agree against Mark in transposing a narrative. Luke sometimes deserts the order of Mark, and Matthew often does so; but in these cases Mark is always supported by the remaining Gospel." [1]

With little qualification this may be accepted as a correct description of the facts, and it admirably proves that there existed what Dr. E. A. Abbott calls an " Original Tradition," to which St. Mark, of the three Evangelists, most closely adhered, giving little else, while St. Matthew and St. Luke borrowed parts of it, [2] combining it with material drawn from other funds of information. But does this prove the kind of *literary* dependence of the first and third Gospels of St. Mark which the current theory supposes ? Or, if dependence exists in any degree, is this the form of theory which most adequately satisfies the conditions ? It is not a question of the *facts*, but one rather of the *interpretation* of the facts. A few reasons may be offered for leaning to a negative answer to the above queries.

---

[1] *Ut supra*, p. 36.

[2] Cf. Abbott, *The Common Tradition of the Synoptic Gospels*, Introd., pp. vi., vii. " To speak more accurately, it is believed that the Gospel of St. Mark contains a closer approximation to the Original Tradition than is contained in the other Synoptics."

1. The impression undeniably produced by agreement in the character and order of the sections in the Gospels is seriously weakened when account is taken of the *widely divergent phraseology* in large parts of the resembling narratives. The divergence is so marked, and so often apparently without motive, that, notwithstanding frequent assonances in words and clauses, a direct borrowing of one Evangelist from another seems next to incredible. The narratives of the Resurrection are a palmary example,[1] but the same thing is observable throughout. Mr. Burkitt has been heard on the agreements ; let Alford state the facts that make for literary independence. " Let any passage," he says, " common to the three Evangelists be put to the test. The phenomena presented will be much as follows · first, perhaps, we shall have three, five, or more words *identical;* then as many *wholly distinct;* then two clauses or more expressed in the same words but *differing order;* then a clause contained in one or two, and *not in the third;* then *several words identical;* then a clause or two not only *wholly distinct* but *apparently inconsistent;* and so forth ; with recurrences of the same arbitrary and anomalous alterations, coincidences, and transpositions."[2] A simple way of testing this state-

---

[1] See the words of Strauss quoted earlier (pp. 59–60).
[2] *Greek Testament*, i. Prol. p. 5.

ment is to take such a book as Dr. Abbott's *The Common Tradition of the Synoptic Gospels*, where the narratives are arranged in parallel columns, and verbal agreements of the *three* Evangelists (the so-called " Triple Tradition " ; the " Double Tradition," can be obtained by underlining in pencil) are indicated in black type, and note the proportion of agreement to divergence in the different sections. The proportion varies, but in most cases the amount of divergence will be found to be very considerable. Dr. Abbott himself goes so far as to say : " Closely though the Synoptists in some passages agree, yet the independence of their testimony requires in these days [as recently as 1884] no proof. Few reasonable sceptics now assert . . . that any of the three first Evangelists had before him the work of the other two. Proof, if proof were needed, might easily be derived from a perusal of the pages of the following Harmony, which would show a number of divergences, half-agreements, incomplete statements, omissions, incompatible, as a whole, with the hypothesis of borrowing." [1]

It cannot be said that the difficulties created by these remarkable phenomena have, up to the present time, been successfully overcome by the advocates of the dependence theory. Dr. A. Wright, in contending for an original " oral " Mark,

[1] *Ut supra*, Introd. p. vi.

thinks they have not yet been removed.[1] Sir
John Hawkins, though he argues for a use of St.
Mark, yet draws attention to a large series of phenomena which he declares to be, " on the whole, and
when taken together, inexplicable on any exclu-
sively or mainly documentary theory."   " Copying
from documents," he says, " does not seem to
account for them : but it is not at all difficult to
see how they might have arisen in the course of oral
transmission." [2] To bring the phenomena into
harmony with the theory of literary dependence
on St. Mark there is needed the assumption of a
freedom in the use of sources by St. Matthew and
St. Luke which passes all reasonable bounds, and
commonly admits of no satisfactory explanation.
" The Evangelists," says Mr. Burkitt, " altered
freely the earlier sources which they used as the

---

[1] Cf. his *Synopsis of the Gospels in Greek,* Introd. p. x.
" At present the hypothesis of a Ur-Markus having been
discredited and practically abandoned, the supporters of
documents insist—in spite (as I think) of the very serious
difficulties which they have not yet removed—that St.
Mark's Gospel was used by St. Matthew and St. Luke."
He points out elsewhere the difficulties of supposing that
St. Luke used St. Mark (p. xvi.).   Dr. Wright's own theory
of a proto-, deutero-, and trito-Mark is loaded with many
difficulties.

[2] *Horae Synopticae,* p. 52. The instances given in Pt.
iv., sects. ii., iii., include variations in the reports of the
sayings of Jesus, the attribution of the same, or similar
words, to different speakers, the use of the same, or similar
words, as parts of a speech, and as part of the Evangelist's
narrative, transpositions, etc.

basis of their narratives." [1]   This freedom of theirs
is then used as proof that " literary piety is a
quality. . . which hardly makes its appearance in
Christendom before 150 A.D." [2] With doubtful
consistency the same writer declares that, if the
Evangelists had worked on a " fixed oral tradition,"
he " cannot imagine how they dared to take such
liberties with it " ! [3]   That is, a " fixed tradition "
is sacred, and dare not be tampered with, but a
document *embodying* this tradition, even though
by a writer like St. Mark, is liable to the freest
literary manipulation ! It is to be remembered
that the proof of the alleged lack of " literary
piety " is mainly the assumption itself that St.
Mark *was* used by the other Evangelists.

2. Assuming, however, some degree of dependence
in the relations of the Gospels, the question is still
pertinent—Is the theory of dependence on St.
Mark *that which alone, or best, satisfies the conditions ?*
It has not always been thought that it is, and very
competent scholars, on grounds that seem cogent,
take the liberty of doubting it still. It is almost
with amused interest that one, in these days, reads
the lengthy and learned argumentation of a Baur,
a Strauss, a Dr. S. Davidson,[4] to demonstrate from

---

[1] *Ut supra*, p. 18.   [2] P. 15.
[3] P. 35.   Elsewhere he bases an argument on St. Luke's
" literary good faith " (p. 118).
[4] Cf. Strauss, *New Life of Jesus*, i. pp. 169–83 ;   S.
Davidson, *Introd. to New Testament*, i. pp. 278 ff., etc.

the textual phenomena that St. Mark was the *latest* of the three Gospels, and depended on St. Matthew and St. Luke, not they on St. Mark.[1] The very phenomena now relied on to prove the originality of St. Mark, e.g., his picturesqueness, are turned by these writers into an argument against him. The argument from verbal coincidences is reversed, and St. Mark is made out to be based on the others because in numerous instances St. Mark's text agrees partly with St. Matthew and partly with St. Luke. And, assuredly, if dependence is assumed, lists can easily be furnished in which the secondary character of the text of St. Mark can as plausibly be maintained. But the Tübingen theory of St. Mark's dependence is by no means the only alternative to the prevailing view. The learned Professor Zahn, e.g., strikes out on a different line, and supposes a dependence of St. Mark on the *Aramaic* St. Matthew, but, conversely, a partial dependence of the *Greek* St. Matthew on

---

[1] More recently, the dependence of St. Mark on St. Matt. and St. Luke is upheld by an able scholar, Dr. Colin Campbell, whose work, *The First Three Gospels in Greek, arranged in Parallel Columns* (second edition, 1899), is designed to support this thesis. In a recent communication Dr. C. writes : " I have seen nothing yet to alter my conviction as to the substantial truth [of this hypothesis] . . . Every detail I have accumulated—and I have a large mass of material—convinces me that the prevalent view is wrong. . . . There are multitudes of expressions in Mark which are best understood if we presuppose his use of Matthew and Luke." (Pages of instances are given.)

the canonical St. Mark.[1] It is, in short, yet too early to take the dependence on St. Mark as a fixed result.

3. A strong argument against the current theory seems to the present writer to arise from *St. Luke's Prologue*,[2] in which the principles which guided the Evangelist in the composition of his Gospel are explicitly laid down. It is to be noted that, in this Preface, St. Luke assumes that the chief matters he is about to relate are already well known —fully established ($\pi\epsilon\pi\lambda\eta\rho o\phi o\rho\eta\mu\acute{\epsilon}\nu\omega\nu$)—in the churches; that they had been received from those who "from the beginning were eye-witnesses ($a\mathrm{\mathring{v}}\tau\acute{o}\pi\tau a\iota$) and ministers of the word"; that they had been the subject of careful catechetical instruction ($\kappa a\tau\eta\chi\acute{\eta}\theta\eta s$); that many attempts had already been made to draw up written narratives of these things. For himself St. Luke claims that he has "traced the course of all things accurately from the first," and his object in writing, as he says, "in order" ($\kappa a\theta\epsilon\xi\hat{\eta} s$), is that Theophilus may "fully know" ($\mathrm{\mathring{\epsilon}}\pi\iota\gamma\nu\hat{\omega} s$) the "certainty" ($a\sigma\phi\acute{a}$$\lambda\epsilon\iota a\nu$) of those things concerning which he had already been orally instructed. Does this, it may be asked, suggest such a process of composition

---

[1] *Einleitung*, ii. pp. 322 ff.

[2] Luke i. 1–4; cf. on this point Dr. A. Wright, *St. Luke's Gospel in Greek*, pp. xiv., xv.; *Synopsis of Gospels in Greek*, p. xviii.

as the current theory supposes ? St. Luke speaks, indeed, of "many" who had taken in hand to draw up written narratives. He alludes to these earlier attempts, not disparagingly, but evidently as implying that they were unauthoritative, lacked order, and generally were unfitted for the purpose his own Gospel was intended to serve. He himself, in contrast with the "many," goes back to first-hand sources, and writes "in order." He is not appropriating the work of others, but drawing from his own researches.[1] How does this tally with the hypothesis now in vogue ? On this hypothesis another principal Gospel not only existed, but was known to St. Luke, and was used by him as a main basis of his own. This Gospel was the work of John Mark, son of Mary of Jerusalem, companion of St. Peter ; therefore may be presumed to have been of high authority. St. Luke sets such value on St. Mark's Gospel that he takes up fully two-thirds of its contents into his own—draws from it, in fact, nearly all his narrative material. He relies so much on its "order" that in only one or two instances does he venture to deviate from it. Does this harmonize with the account he himself

---

[1] Dr. Wright says : "His authorities were not written documents, but partly eye-witnesses, partly professional catechists" (ut supra). Dr. Plummer says : "That [the reference to 'eye-witnesses'] would at once exclude Matthew, whose Gospel Luke does not appear to have known. It is doubtful whether Mark is included in the πολλοί."

gives? The linguistic phenomena in St. Luke, which show a far wider divergence from the Marcan type than in the first Gospel, again present difficulties.[1] On the other hand, the "order," which appears to belong to the form which the narratives had come to assume before any Gospel was written,[2] cannot alone be relied on to prove dependence, and singular *omissions* remain to be accounted for.[3]

On the whole, therefore, it appears safer not to allow a theory of dependence to rule the treatment, or to create an initial prejudice against one Gospel in comparison with another. St. Matthew and St. Luke may be heard without assuming that either Gospel, in its narrative portions, is a simple echo of St. Mark.

It is impossible here to enter on the grounds which, it is believed, justify the view that the Fourth Gospel is a genuine work of the Apostle

[1] Cf. Wright, *Synopsis*, p. xvi.

[2] In all the Synoptics certain groups or chains of events are linked together in the same way, evidently as the result of traditional connexion. E.g., the Cure of the Paralytic, the Call and Feast of Matthew, Questionings of Pharisees and of John's Disciples ; again, the Plucking of the Ears of Corn, the Cure of the Man with the Withered Hand (Sabbath Stories). St. Matthew frequently transposes, in the interests of his own plan—chiefly, however, in the *earlier* part of his Gospel.

[3] Cf. Burkitt, p. 130 : "He freely omits large portions of Mark," etc. One important series in St. Matthew (xiv., 22–xvi. 12) and St. Mark (vi. 45–viii. 26) is, for no obvious reason, wholly omitted in St. Luke.

John,[1] containing authentic reminiscences of that Apostle of the Lord's doings and teachings, especially in Judæa, and in His more intimate intercourse with His disciples, thus filling up the outline of the other Evangelists in places which they had left blank.[2] The difficulty which weighs so strongly with Mr. Burkitt of finding a place in the framework of St. Mark for the Raising of Lazarus is certainly not insuperable ; [3] while his own view of the free invention of this and other incidents and discourses by the Evangelist [4] deprives the Gospel of even the slightest claim to historical credit. But the whole tone of the Gospel suggests a writer who has minute and accurate knowledge of the matters about which he writes—down even to small personal details—and who *means* to be taken as a faithful witness.[5]   As such he is accepted here.

[1] Reference may simply be made to the works of Principal Drummond and Dr. Sanday on the Fourth Gospel. Mr. Burkitt is hard driven when he relies on the late and untrustworthy references to Papias to overturn the unanimous early tradition of St. John's residence in Ephesus (p. 252).

[2] Mr. Burkitt doubts if our Synoptic Gospels contain stories from more than forty separate days of our Lord's life (p. 20).   [3] Cf. pp. 222-3, and Pref. to second edition.

[4] " If [Mark] did not know of it [The Raising of Lazarus], can we believe that, as a matter of fact, it ever occurred ? " Cf. pp. 225-6, 237, etc.

[5] The interesting treatment of "The Historical Problems of the Fourth Gospel," from a lay point of view, in R. H. Hutton's *Theological Essays*, well deserves attention at the present time.

The way is now open for the consideration of the application of these critical theories to the narratives of the Resurrection, and attention may first be given to certain features in the accounts of the Resurrection itself.

At first sight, nothing might seem plainer than that the narratives of the first three Gospels, while necessarily related, are yet *independent*, in the sense that no one of them is copied from, or based on, the others. As already hinted, the difficulties of a theory of dependence are here at their maximum. In scarcely any particular—time, names and number of women, events at the grave, number, appearance and position of angels, etc.—do their accounts exactly agree. This is indeed the stronghold of the argument from " discrepancies " of which so much is made. The theory, however, is, that the narratives in St. Matthew and St. Luke are derived from the simpler story of St. Mark ; and in carrying through this theory the advocates of dependence are driven to the most arbitrary and complicated hypotheses to explain how the divergences arose. It will be interesting to watch the process of dissolving the credit of the narratives by the aid of this assumption in the skilled hands of a writer like Professor Lake—though the result may rather appear as a *reductio ad absurdum* of the theory itself.

To begin with, certain cases of omission of details

by St. Matthew and St. Luke are proposed to be solved by the hypothesis of an " original Mark " (*Ur-Markus*), from which these details were absent. Professor Lake, while not committing himself to the theory, which Dr. Wright tells us is now " discredited and practically abandoned," [1] yet so far inclines to it that he thinks—the reader will note the *simplicity* of the hypothesis—" there is something to be said for the view that the original Marcan document did not give any names in Mark xv. 47, and that this form was used by Luke ; [2] that a later edition, used by Matthew, identified the women as Mary Magdalene and the other Mary ; and that another editor produced the text which is found in the canonical Mark." [3]

More serious, however, is the difficulty that the narratives are frequently divergent in phraseology and circumstance in what they *do* relate. How is this to be explained ? To take a leading example, St. Mark narrates of the women that " entering into the tomb, they saw a young man sitting on the right side, arrayed in a white robe." [4] St. Matthew has an independent story of a great earthquake, and represents an angel as rolling away the stone and sitting upon it.[5] St. Luke records that,

---

[1] *Synopsis*, p. x.
[2] It is a difficulty that St. Luke so often omits the proper names in St. Mark. Cf. Wright, *ut supra*.
[3] Lake, *ut supra*, p. 54.
[4] Mark. xvi. 5. [5] Matt. xxviii. 2–5.

when they had entered the tomb, " two men stood
by them in dazzling apparel." [1]   No divergence
could be greater, on the principle that " the two
other Gospels, Matthew and Luke, are closely based
on the Marcan narrative." [2]   But Professor Lake
is not discouraged. Accepting St. Mark's narrative as the original, " the others," he thinks, " all
fall into place on an intelligible though complicated
system of development under the influence of
known causes." [3]   " Complicated " indeed—and
unreal—as will be seen by glancing at it.

First, there is a slight (infinitesimal) possibility
that the Marcan text may originally have read,
" came to the tomb " (instead of " entered into "), [4]
and this left it doubtful whether the " young man "
of the story was seen " on the right side " *inside*
or *outside* the tomb. [5]   In " elucidating " the point
left in ambiguity, St. Luke took it the one way and
St. Matthew the other—hence their variation.
Only, if this is not the correct reading, the explanation falls.

Next, the " young man " in St. Mark " appears
without any explanation of his identity or mission." [6]   He was really, on Professor Lake's theory,
as will be seen later, a youth at the spot who tried
to persuade the women that they had come to the

---

[1] Luke xxiv. 3–5.   [2] *Ut supra*, p. 63.
[3] P. 62–3.   [4] The Vat MS. reads ἐλθοῦσαι.
[5] *Ut supra*, pp. 62–3.   [6] P. 184.

wrong tomb.[1] Naturally, however, attempts were soon made to identify him. " The most obvious view for that generation, in which angelology was so powerful a force, was that he was an angel. This view is adopted in Matthew."[2] " Still a further step is to be found in the doubling of the angel, again strictly in accordance with Jewish thought." This in St. Luke, St. John, and the Gospel of Peter.[3] " Why are there two men in Luke instead of one ? The answer is not quite plain, but it seems probable that there was a general belief in Jewish and possibly other circles that two angels were specially connected with the messages of God."[4] Elsewhere the probability is conceded that St. Luke is here following a different tradition from St. Mark's.[5] But why, then, not all through ?

We are not done yet, however, with this " young man " of St. Mark's narrative. An attempt is made " to bring together and trace the development of the various forms in which the original ' young man ' is represented in various books."[6] " Two hypotheses," we are told, " naturally presented themselves : one that the young man was an angel ; the other that he was the Risen Lord Himself."[7] St. Matthew, after his manner, adopted both views. The angel sitting on the stone is one form : the appearance of Jesus to the women as

[1] Cf. pp. 251-2.   [2] P. 185.   [3] P. 185.
[4] P. 67.   [5] Pp. 67, 92.   [6] P. 67.   [7] P. 85.

they went [1] is the other. This appearance of
Jesus recorded by St. Matthew is held to be a
" doublet " of St. Mark's young man story. So
is St. John's account of the appearance of the Lord
to Mary Magdalene.[2]

If attention has been given to this incident in
some detail, it is because, in its far-fetched conjectures and hypothetical ingenuities, it represents
so characteristically the processes by which it is
sought to dissipate the credibility of the Gospel
narratives, and the methods by which the Marcan
theory is applied to this end. The real effect of
its forced combinations and toppling structure " of
possibles " and " perhapses " is to cast doubt on
the theory with which it starts, and lend strength
to the view of the independence of the narratives.
After all, why should St. Luke, whose narrative is
so very divergent, be supposed to be dependent on
St. Mark in his account of the Resurrection ? Professor Lake has been heard admitting that it is
possible that St. Luke followed a different tradition.
Going a stage further back, we find Mr. Burkitt
allowing that St. Luke in the Passion " deserts
Mark to follow another story of the last scenes." [3]
At the other end, St. Luke is admittedly original
in his account of the *post*-Resurrection appearances.

---

[1] P. 85, Matt. xxviii. 9.
[2] P. 186, John xx. 14, 15.
[3] *Ut supra*, p. 130.

Why then should he not be so in the narrative of the Resurrection itself? The same question may be asked regarding St. Matthew. The harmonistic expedients censured in commentators are mild in comparison with the violence needed to evolve the narratives of either of the other Evangelists out of that of St. Mark.

The detailed examination of the narratives next to be undertaken will further illustrate the untenableness of the new critical constructions, and provide the basis of a positive argument for the reality of the Resurrection.

THE CREDIBILITY OF THE WITNESS—
THE BURIAL

IV

THE CREDIBILITY OF THE WITNESS—THE BURIAL

ONE of the most touching scenes in Goethe's *Faust* is where the heart-sick sceptic, about to drain the poison-goblet, is turned from his purpose by hearing the ringing of the Easter bells, and the choral hymns, proclaiming that the Lord is risen. " I hear your message," is his first comment, " but I have not faith. Miracle is faith's favourite child."[1] In this we hear the voice of to-day. But the sweet sounds, with their tidings of victory and joy for the world, melt and conquer—for the time.

> Sing ye on, sweet songs that are of heaven !
> Tears come, Earth has her child again.

It is this " Easter Message," fraught with such infinite consolation for mankind, which is again placed in question. The mood of the sceptic is resumed. Faith may, if it will, believe that Jesus lives with God ; that He has not in spirit succumbed to death. But the historical fact on which the Church has hitherto reposed its confidence in His

[1] " Das Wunder ist des Glaubens liebstes Kind."

victory over death—His Resurrection in the body from the grave—is negatived as incredible, and the evidence on which the belief rests is declared to be valueless as proof of so great a wonder. A little has already been said of the methods by which the breaking down of the evidence is attempted on the part of historical criticism. Much is made of the secondary character of the narratives, of their contradictions, of the mythical and legendary elements alleged to be apparent in them. The accounts are pitted against each other, are picked to pieces, and attacked in their separate details (" divide and conquer.").[1] Their larger coherences, the connexion with the life of Christ as a whole, their antecedents and consequents in revelation and history—all this is left out of view or minimized. It is time to come to closer quarters with this bold challenge of the evidence, and to ask how far the denial rests on satisfactory grounds.

One or two general remarks are pertinent at the outset.

It is customary to urge as decisive against the narratives of the Gospels that not any of the writers are first-hand witnesses. This, however, as already hinted, is to take much too narrow a view. If the

[1] Cf., amongst recent works, *Die Auferstehung Christi*, by Arnold Meyer (1905), and the work of Prof. Lake repeatedly referred to, *The Historical Evidence for the Resurrection of Jesus Christ*. (Now Abbé Loisy's *Les Évangiles Synoptiques*.)

Fourth Gospel, as is here presumed, and as indications in its Resurrection narratives themselves tend to show, is a genuine work of the Apostle John, we have one witness of foremost rank who *was* an eye-witness. St. Mark, according to a tradition which there seems no reason to doubt, was the " interpreter " of St. Peter [1]—another primary witness. St. Luke lays stress upon the fact that the things which he relates rested primarily on the testimony of those " which from the beginning were eye-witnesses and ministers of the word." [2] The Gospel of St. Matthew, if not directly the work of that Apostle, must have been written by one in such close intimacy with the Apostle—another first-hand witness—that his Gospel ever after passed as St. Matthew's own.[3] St Paul's appeal is to eye-witnesses.[4]

But there is more than this. It is never to be forgotten that, as the words of St. Luke above cited imply, the writers of the Synoptical Gospels, like Confucius in China, were not " originators " but " transmitters." Their business was not to create, but simply to record, as faithfully as they could,

[1] Papias, in Eusebius, *Ecc. Hist.* iii. 39, and generally in the ancient Church. Cf. Meyer, Weiss, Westcott, Salmon, Zahn, etc.

[2] Luke i. 2.

[3] Cf. Zahn, *Einleitung*, ii. 259. All early writers agree in accepting the Greek Gospel as St. Matthew's, even while declaring that he wrote in Aramaic.

[4] 1 Cor. xv. 5–8.

a tradition already existing and well established in the Church—a tradition derived originally from Apostles, circulating in oral and written form, and well preserved by careful catechetical teaching. It is to be remembered that the Apostles, with numerous other eye-witnesses, lived for years together at Jerusalem, continuously engaged in the work of instruction; that during this period they were in constant communication with each other, with their converts, and with the Churches which they founded; that the witness which they bore necessarily acquired a fixed and familiar form; and that the deposit of the common tradition which we have in the Gospels has behind it, in its main features, all the weight of this consentient testimony—is, therefore, of the highest value as evidence. If it is not the testimony of this or that single eye-witness, it may be something better.

Next, as to the " contradictions." These, it will be seen immediately, are greatly exaggerated. But even on the points which present undeniable difficulties, certain things, in fairness, are to be borne in mind. We see how minute, faithful, and life-like are the narratives of the Lord's Crucifixion. The events of the Resurrection morning could not be less well known. The Apostles were, above all things else, witnesses to the Resurrection.[1] Within a few weeks of the Crucifixion they were proclaim-

[1] Acts. i. 22, ii. 32, iii. 15, iv. 33 ; i Cor. xv. 15.

ing the Resurrection of Jesus in the streets of Jerusalem, and making multitudes of converts by their preaching.[1] The facts must have been constantly talked about, narrated in preaching, experiences compared, particular incidents connected with this or that person or group of persons, either as original informants, or as prominent persons in the story. It is further to be remembered that the Resurrection day was necessarily one of great excitement. Events and experiences, as the tale was told, would be mingled, blended, grouped, in a way which no one who was not an eye-witness, like St. John, would be able afterwards clearly to disentangle. Yet the essential facts, and even the chief details of the story, would stand out beyond all reasonable question. This is what we would expect in the narratives of the Gospels, and what, in fact, we find. No one of the Evangelists professes to give a complete account of everything that happened on that wonderful Easter morning and day. Each selects and combines from his own point of view; gives outstanding names and facts, without disputing or denying that others may have something else to tell; in default of more exact knowledge, sometimes generalizes. It is here that St. John, with his more precise and consecutive narration, affords valuable aid,[2] as he

[1] Acts ii.–iv.
[2] It is possible to agree with Renan here. " In all that

does so frequently in matters of chronology in the Gospels.

In narratives of this description, however credible in origin and substance, it is clearly as hopeless as it is unfair to adopt the methods of a pettifogging attorney, bent at all costs on tripping the witness up on small details. No two of the Evangelists, e.g., agree precisely in the terms they employ as to the time of the visit of the women to the tomb.[1] Yet in all four it is plainly implied that the visit took place in early morning, when dawn was merging into day, and that it was full daylight before the visit was completed. One Evangelist names certain women ; others add a name or two more. —names familiar in all the accounts. How small such points are as the basis of a charge of irreconcilable contradictions! How few statements of public events, even where stricter accuracy of expression is aimed at, could endure to have such methods applied to them ![2]

concerns the narrative of the Resurrection and the appearances," he says, "the Fourth Gospel maintains that superiority which it has for all the rest of the Life of Jesus. If we wish to find a consecutive logical narrative, which allows that which is hidden behind the allusions to be conjectured, it is there that we must look for it " (Les Apôtres, p. ix.). Attention may again be drawn to R. H. Hutton's essay on " The Historical Problems of the Fourth Gospel " (Theol. Essays, No. vii.).

[1] On this and the next example, see after.

[2] Critics are always girding at the doctrine of " verbal inspiration." Yet their own objections rest on the postu-

Two examples may illustrate.

Professor Huxley was a man of scientific mind, from whom accurate statement in an ordinary narrative of fact might justly be expected. It happens, however, that in Huxley's *Darwiniana* the scientist makes two references in different papers to the origin of the breed of Ancon sheep. It is instructive to put the two passages side by side.

Here is the first :—

With the 'cuteness characteristic of their nation, the neighbours of the Massachusetts farmer imagined that it would be an excellent thing if all his sheep were imbued with the stay-at-home tendencies enforced by Nature on the newly-arrived ram, and they advised Wright to kill the old patriarch of his fold, and instal the Ancon ram in his place. The result justified their sagacious anticipations.[1]

Here is the other :—

It occurred to Seth Wright, who was, like his successors, more or less 'cute, that if he could get a stock of sheep like those with the bandy legs, they would not be able to jump over the fences so readily ; and he acted upon that idea.[2]

Here, manifestly, are " discrepancies " which, on critical principles, should discredit the whole story. In the latter narrative we have Seth Wright alone ; in the former, neighbours ; [" the second

late of the narrowest view of verbal inspiration, and lose their force on any other hypothesis.

[1] *Darwiniana*, pp. 38-9.   [2] P. 409.

narrative," we might say in the usual style, "knows nothing of neighbours;" the longer version is plainly a later expansion]. In the latter, the idea is Seth Wright's very own—the product of his own 'cuteness; in the other, the 'cuteness is wholly in the neighbours, and Seth Wright only acts on their advice. Yet how contemptuously would any sensible person scout such hypercriticism!

A second instructive example is furnished in a recent issue of the *Bibliotheca Sacra*.[1] A class in history was studying the French Revolution, and the pupils were asked to look the matter up, and report next day by what vote Louis XVI was condemned. Nearly half the class reported that the vote was unanimous. A considerable number protested that he was condemned by a majority of one. A few gave the majority as 145 in a vote of 721. "How utterly irreconcilable these reports seemed! Yet for each the authority of reputable historians could be given. In fact, all were true, and the full truth was a combination of all three." On the first vote as to the king's guilt there was no contrary voice. Some tell only of this. The vote on the penalty was given individually, with reasons, and a majority of 145 declared for the death penalty, at once or after peace was made with Austria, or after confirmation by the people. The votes for

---

[1] Oct., 1907, pp. 768-9

immediate death were only 361 as against 360. History abounds with similar illustrations.[1]

It helps, further, to set this question in its right light, if it is kept in mind that the Gospel narratives take for granted the Resurrection of Jesus as a fact universally accepted, on Apostolic testimony, and aim primarily, not at proof of the fact, but at telling how the event came about, and was brought on that Easter morning to the knowledge of the disciples, with the surprising consequences. It is not evidence led in a court of law, but information concerning an event which everybody already knew and believed in, which they furnish. This explains, in part, their naïve and informal character. It reminds us also that, while the value of these narratives, as contributing to the evidence of the fact, cannot be exaggerated, the certainty of the fact itself rests on a prior and much broader basis— the unfaltering Apostolic witness.[2] The origin of

[1] As an example of another kind, reference may be made to Rev. R. J. Campbell's volume of *Sermons Addressed to Individuals*, where, on pp. 145–6 and pp. 181–2 the same story of a Brighton man is told with affecting dramatic details. The story is no doubt true in substance ; but for " discrepancies "—let the reader compare them, and never speak more (or Mr. Campbell either) of the Gospels !

[2] As shown in a previous paper, the *belief* in the Resurrection is admitted on all hands. R. Otto, in his *Leben und Wirken Jesu*, says : " It can be firmly maintained : no fact in history is better attested than, not indeed the Resurrection, but certainly the rock-fast conviction of the

the Christian Church, it will hereafter be argued, can simply not be explained except on the assumption of the reality of the fact. Meanwhile it is to be inquired what credit attaches to the Gospel relation of the circumstances of this astonishing event which has changed the whole outlook of the generations of mankind upon the future.

Let the chief points be taken in order, and their credibility examined. The force of the objections of a destructive historical criticism can then be tested.

A first fact attested by all the witnesses is that *Jesus died and was buried.* St. Paul sums up the unanimous belief of the early Church on this point in the words : " That Christ died for our sins according to the Scriptures, and that He was buried." [1] The reality of Christ's death, as against the swoon theories, was touched on before, and need not be re-argued. No one now holds that Jesus did *not* die !

" He was buried," St. Paul says. How He was buried is told by the Evangelists. The facts must have been perfectly well known to the primitive community, and the accounts in all four Gospels, as might be expected, are in singular agreement.[2]

first community of the Resurrection of Christ " (p. 49). It is here contended that the belief is inexplicable, under the conditions, without the fact.

[1] I Cor. xv. 3, 4. ;

[2] Matt. xxvii. 57–61 ; Mark xv. 42–7 ; Luke xxiii. 50–6 ; John xix. 38 42.

Combining their statements, we learn that Joseph
of Arimathæa, an honourable councillor (Mark and
John), and secret disciple of Jesus (Matthew, John),
a " rich man " (Matthew), one " looking for the
kingdom of God " (Mark, Luke), " a good man and
a righteous " (Luke), begged from Pilate the body
of Jesus (all four), and, wrapping it in a linen cloth
(all), buried it in a new (Matthew, Luke, John)
rock-tomb (all) belonging to himself (Matthew, cf.
John), in the vicinity of the place of crucifixion (in
" a garden," John says), and closed the entrance
with a great (Matthew, Mark, implied in the others)
stone. St. John further informs us that Nicodemus
assisted in the burial, bringing with him costly
spices. Phraseology differs in the accounts, and
slight particulars furnished by our Evangelist are
lacking or unnoticed in the others. St. Mark alone,
e.g., tells of Pilate's hesitation in granting Joseph's
request, and alone relates that Joseph " bought "
a linen cloth. Yet the story, on the face of it, is
harmonious throughout, and what any Evangelist
fails to state the rest of his narrative generally
implies. St. Luke and St. John do not even mention the rolling of the stone to the door of the tomb
(the fact was one so well known that it could be
omitted). But it is told how the stone was found
removed on the Resurrection morning.[1]

What has historical criticism to say to this story ?

---

[1] Luke xxiv. 2 ; John xx. 1.

One method is simply to deny or ignore it, and to aver, in teeth of the evidence, that the body of Jesus was probably cast by the Jews to the dung-hill,[1] or otherwise disposed of. This, however, is generally felt to be too drastic a procedure, and the tendency in recent criticism has been to accept the main fact of Joseph's interment of the body of Jesus,[2] but usually with qualifications and explanations which deprive the act of the character it has in the Gospels. Professor Lake's book may again serve to illustrate the process. According to this writer, the narrative which, to the ordinary eye, reads so harmoniously is honeycombed with contradictions. The variations and omissions in the accounts form, indeed, a difficulty in the way of the Marcan theory—e.g., the omission of St. Mark's mention of the hesitation of Pilate (Matthew, Luke), or of the names of the women at the tomb (Luke) —but this is got over, or minimized, by the suggestion of an " Ur-Markus." [3] Then the path is open to assume that St. Matthew's " rich man," and St.

---

[1] Thus Strauss, Réville, etc. Réville, quoted by Godet, says the Jews perhaps cast the body of Jesus on the dust-heap, and adds, " as was generally done with the bodies of executed criminals." Godet points out that " such a custom was not in conformity with Jewish or Roman law " (*Defence of the Christian Faith*, E. T., p. 106).

[2] Thus Renan, H. J. Holtzmann, O. Holtzmann, Prof. Lake, etc. Strauss allows that Roman law permitted the handing over of the body to friends (*Ulpian*, xlviii. 24).

[3] *Res. of Jesus Christ*, pp. 52—4.

Luke's " good man and righteous," are but varying interpretations (" paraphrases ") of St. Mark's " a councillor of honourable estate " ; [1] that the discipleship of St. Matthew, said to be unknown to, and in contradiction with, St. Mark, is an attempt to find a " motive " for the burial ; [2] that St. Luke, by the use of the term " hewn in stone " ($\lambda a \xi \epsilon \acute{v} \tau \omega$) contradicts the description of the tomb in the other Synoptics ; [3] while St. John goes still further astray in regarding the tomb as " a kind of mausoleum," [4] etc. " The discipleship ascribed to Joseph in John [as in Matthew] is not really to be reconciled with the Marcan account." [5] The probable truth is held to be that Joseph, a member of the Sanhedrim, and acting as its representative,[6] was moved to do what he did solely by regard for the precept in Deuteronomy xxi. 22 ff. : that the body of a criminal hanged on a tree should be buried before sunset.[7]

But how far-fetched and distorted is all this theorizing ! The contradictions in the narratives

---

[1] Pp. 50–1.   [2] Pp. 46, 50, 61, 173, etc.

[3] P. 51. " In Mark we have an ordinary rock-tomb ; in Luke, a tomb of hewn stone ; in John, a mausoleum with a place for the body in the centre " (p. 176).

[4] Pp. 172–3.   [5] Pp. 172.

[6] Pp. 177, 182. Mr. Burkitt, on the other hand, seems to question that $\beta o u \lambda \acute{\eta} \tau \eta s$ means a member of the Sanhedrim, and hints that St. Luke has here again mistaken St. Mark (Gospel History, p. 56). There is no reason to doubt St. Luke's accuracy in his understanding of the word.

[7] Pp. 130, 182.

hunted out with such painstaking zeal simply do not exist. To take first the question of discipleship. If the *word* " disciple " is not used by St. Mark and St. Luke, is not the *fact* of discipleship to the degree intended—a secret sympathy now coming to avowal—written across their narratives as plainly as across those of St. Matthew and St. John ? What else but discipleship of this kind could move a member of the Sanhedrim (" he had not," St. Luke tells us, " consented to their counsel and deed." [1]), on the very day of Christ's crucifixion, to come boldly forward (" having dared," St. Mark says [2]), to ask from Pilate the body of the Crucified ; . then, having bought linen, to wrap it therein and give it reverent burial in a rock-tomb (according to St. Matthew, his own ; [3] according to St. Matthew, St. Luke, St. John,[4] new) ?   Indeed, does not the very expression used by St. Mark and St. Luke, " looking for the kingdom of God," imply, *for them*, a measure of discipleship ?

Is it probable, Professor Lake asks, that a disciple would have been a member of the Sanhedrim, or

---

[1] Luke xxiii. 51.   [2] Mark xv. 43.   [3] Matt. xxvii. 60.
[4] Matt. xvii. 60 ;   Luke xxiii. 53 ; John xix. 41.   " In the first Gospel," says Strauss, " Joseph is a disciple of Jesus—and such must have been the man who, under circumstances so unfavourable, did not hesitate to take charge of His body " (*Life of Jesus*, iii. p. 297).   Renan follows the narratives without hesitation, including the anointing (*Vie de Jésus*, chap. xxvi.).

have omitted the anointing ?[1] " If Joseph was not a disciple, he probably did not anoint the body, if he was, he probably did."[2] Then the absence of the mention of the anointing in St. Mark is taken as a proof that Joseph was not a disciple. But in St. Matthew's narrative, where the discipleship is asserted, there is no anointing either. On Professor Lake's showing, it should nevertheless be presupposed.[3] " Mark says that Joseph was a member of the Sanhedrim, and that he did not anoint the body."[4] St. Mark makes no such statement. What Professor Lake converts into this assertion is an inference of his own from a later part of the narrative, where St. Mark speaks of the purchase of spices by the women with a view to *their* anointing on the first day of the week.[5]

The attempt to make out a discrepancy about the tomb is even less successful. In the adjective $\lambda a \xi \epsilon \upsilon \tau \omega$ in St. Luke Professor Lake seems to have discovered a signification unknown to most students of the language. One asks, by what right does he impose on this word, occurring here alone in the New Testament, a sense contrary to that of the corresponding

---

[1] *Ut supra*, p. 171.   [2] P. 173.
[3] In another place he says, " He [Matthew] had given an explanation of the burial by Joseph of Arimathæa—discipleship—which rendered it improbable that the latter had omitted the usual last kindnesses to a dead friend's body " (p. 61). St. Matthew should at least be cleared of contradiction to St. John.
[4] P. 171.   [5] Mark xvi. 1.

in which it occurs in the LXX (Deut. iv. 49), it cannot well mean aught else than hewn out of the rock. Meyer appears to give the meaning correctly, " hewn in stone, therefore neither dug nor built." [1] But the tomb, it is objected, was not necessarily Joseph's own, as St. Matthew affirms. Surely, however, the very use of it for the burial of the Lord's body, which all the Evangelists attest, is the strongest of proofs that it was. The tomb was evidently one of some distinction. Three witnesses describe it as " new," " where never man had yet lain " (Matthew, Luke, and John), and it was situated in " a garden." [2] Can those who write thus have thought of it as other than the property of the councillor who used it. Or was it the custom in Judaea for people simply to appropriate any one's rock-tomb that pleased them? [3] Professor Lake finds

[1] *Com. in loc.* On Jewish tombs and burial customs, cf. Latham, *The Risen Master*, pp. 33–6, 87–8, and plates.

[2] John xix. 41.

[3] Cf. Ebrard, *Gospel History*, E. T., p. 446 ; Godet, *Com. on St. John*, E. T., iii. p. 282. O. Holtzmann's theory of the Resurrection, as will be seen later, turns on the very point that the tomb was Joseph's (*Leben Jesu*, p. 392). A. Meyer's conjecture (*Die Auferstehung*, p. 123) that the tomb was a chance, deserted one, not only contradicts the evidence but is out of harmony with St. Mark's narrative of the loving care shown in Christ's burial. The circumstance that St. John gives the proximity of the tomb as a reason for the burial (xix. 42) in no way contra-

a discrepancy even in St. Luke's omitting to mention the closing of the door with a stone ! But he adds in a footnote: " But the stone is implied in Luke xxii. 2. Either St. Luke forgot his previous omission or the latter was, after all, accidental ! " [1]

The futility of the counter-explanation offered of Joseph of Arimathæa's action hardly needs elaboration. Is it credible that any member of the Sanhedrim, without living sympathy with Jesus —still more the Sanhedrim as a body or their representative—should behave in the manner recorded from the simple motive of securing that a criminal who had undergone execution should be buried before sunset ? The answer may be left to the reader's own reflections.

Connected with the burial is the story of *the guard at the tomb*, narrated only by St. Matthew [2]—therefore lacking the breadth of attestation of the main history. It is not, on that account, as is very frequently assumed, to be dismissed as legendary. If it has behind it the authority of St. Matthew, it is certainly not legendary ; even if not his, it may come from some first-hand and quite authentic source. It will fall to be considered again in connexion with the events of the Resurrection. Meanwhile it need only be remarked that its credibility is at least not shaken by many of the objections

---

[1] *Ut supra*, p. 51.
[2] Matt. xxvii. 62–9 ; cf. xxviii. 4, 11–15.

which have been urged against it.[1]   If the Gospel narratives are to be believed, the action, teaching, and miracles of Jesus—including the Resurrection of Lazarus [2]—had made a deep impression on the authorities.   Especially had the events of the past week stirred them to the depths.[3]   Had they not on the previous night condemned Jesus for a blasphemous claim to Messiahship ?   Had not mysterious words of His about the building of the temple in three days been quoted against Him ? [4]   Had the betrayer dropped no hints of sayings of Jesus in which, repeatedly, He had spoken of His being put to death and rising again the third day ? [5]   If such things came to the ears of the chief priests and Pharisees, as it is implied they did, do they not furnish sufficient motive for what followed ?   Herod's conscience-stricken thought about Jesus, that He, was John the Baptist risen from the dead,[6] shows that such ideas as Resurrection were not far to seek.   Even if the guilty consciences of those responsible for Christ's crucifixion prompted no such fears, was not the fact that the body had been com-

---

[1] See these in Meyer's *Com. on Matthew, in loc.*
[2] Cf. John xi. 47–57.
[3] Matt. xxi. 12–16, xxiii., xxvi. 3–5, etc.
[4] Matt. xxvi. 6–1 ; Mark xiv. 58 ; cf. John ii. 18–22.
[5] Matt. xvi. 21 ; xvii. 22, 23 ; xx. 16, 19 (so Mark, Luke). O. Holtzmann accepts and builds upon the genuineness of these sayings (*Leben Jesu*, p. 388).   So earlier, Renan, in part (*Les Apôtres*, ch. i.).
[6] Matt. xlv. 2 ; Mark vi. 14–61 ; Luke ix. 7–9.

mitted to Christ's friends enough to create the
apprehension that His disciples might remove it
and afterwards pretend that He had risen ? It was
with this plea that they went to Pilate and obtained
the watch they sought. To make security doubly
sure, they sealed the tomb with the official seal.
The sole result, under providence, was to afford
new evidence for the reality of the Resurrection.

The events of the Resurrection morning itself
now claim our attention. But a minor point already
alluded to, connecting the Resurrection narratives
with those just considered, viz., the *purpose* attributed to the holy women by two of the Evangelists [1]
of anointing the body of Jesus, may first be touched
on. In regard to it several difficulties (" contradictions ") have been raised.

There is first the supposed inconsistency between
this intention of the women of Galilee and the fact
recorded by St. John alone,[2] that the anointing
had already been done by Joseph and Nicodemus,
with lavish munificence, at the time of burial. The
women were present at that scene.[3] Why then
should they contemplate a repetition of the func-
tion ? Then contradictions are pointed out in the
narratives of the Synoptics themselves, inasmuch as
St. Matthew, from a motive which Professor Lake

[1] Mark xvi. 1 ; Luke xxiii. 56 ; xxiv. 1.
[2] John xix. 39, 40. Strauss elaborates this objection.
Renan finds no difficulty.
[3] Matt. xxvii. 61 ; Mark xv. 49 ; Luke xxiii. 55.

thinks he can divine,[1] omits this feature altogether, while St. Mark places the purchase of the spices on the Saturday (" when the Sabbath was past "),[2] and St. Luke on the Friday [3] evening. Are these difficulties really formidable ? In a fair judgment it is hard to believe it. The difficulty is rather with those who suppose that St. Matthew, with St. Mark's Gospel before him, designedly omitted or changed this particular, or that St. Matthew and St. Luke, both copying from St. Mark, fell into contradiction with each other,[4] and with their source. Grant independent narration, and the difficulties mostly vanish.

With reference to the first point, it should be observed that, in strictness, St. John, in his narrative of the burial, says nothing of " anointing." The " mixture of myrrh and aloes " need not have been an ointment, and the language of the Gospel, "bound it [the body] in linen cloths with the spices,"[5]

---

[1] *Ut supra*, p. 61. The motive, as stated above, is that St. Matthew presupposes an anointing by Joseph. He has also a guard at the tomb. A. Meyer (*Die Auferstehung*, pp. 108, 111) contents himself with the guard.

[2] Mark xvi. 1.   [3] Luke xxiii. 56.

[4] St. Luke is thought to have been ignorant of, or to have momentarily forgotten, the Jewish method of reckoning days—a likely supposition (p. 59). Is it not St. Luke himself who tells us in verse 54 : " And the Sabbath drew on (Greek, " began to dawn ") ?

[5] John xix. 40. Luthardt comments : " Probably of pulverized gum, myrrh and aloe-wood, that was strewn between the bandages " (*Com. in loc.*). St. Luke distin-

suggests that it was not.[1] But not to press this point, the circumstances have to be considered. The burial by Joseph of Arimathæa was extremely hurried. The permission of Pilate had to be obtained, the body taken down, linen and spices bought, the body prepared for burial and interred, all within the space of two or three hours—possibly less.[2] It was probably cleansed, and enswathed within the linen sheet or bandages with the spices, without more being attempted. There was plainly room here for the more loving and complete anointing which the devotion of the women would suggest.[3] Probably this was intended from the first. It is not, at least, surprising that their affection should contemplate such an act, and that steps should immediately be taken, perhaps a beginning of purchases made, to carry out their purpose.

Next, with respect to the alleged Synoptic inconsistencies, Professor Lake being witness, St. Matthew's text, albeit silent, does not exclude, but

guishes, as a physician would, between " spices " and " ointments " (xxiii. 56).

[1] Cf. Latham, *The Risen Master*, pp. 9 (quoting Ellicott), 36–7.

[2] The haste was due to the nearness of the Sabbath (Mark and Luke).

[3] If, in modern custom, wreaths were placed on the grave of a friend in a hurried burial, would this preclude the desire of other mourners, who had not earlier opportunity, to bring *their* wreaths ? or would they carefully reckon up whether enough had not already been done ? Cf. Ebrard, *Gospel History*, p. 446.

presupposes, such an anointing—if anointing it was—as that described by St. John.[1] Much less, surely, can it be held to exclude the intention, recorded in St. Mark and St. Luke, of the women to anoint—a circumstance probably left unnoticed because never carried into effect,[2] or because soon overshadowed by greater events. The point is very immaterial as to when precisely the purchases of spices were made. The "internal probability," as Professor Lake would say, is that the purchases were commenced in the short space that remained before the Sabbath began, and were completed after the Sabbath ended. Most likely some women made purchases at one time, others at another. In stating, however, that "they returned, and prepared spices and ointments,"[3] St. Luke is probably not intending to fix any precise time: perhaps had not the means of doing it. The next verse ["And on the Sabbath they rested, according to the commandment"] as the μέν shows, and the R.V. correctly indicates, begins a new paragraph.

With the narratives of the wonderful events of the Easter morning, which are next to be considered,

[1] *Ut supra*, p. 61.
[2] The reasons assigned by the critics are quite gratuitous. St. Matthew has in view, like the others, an anointing for burial (cf. the story of Mary of Bethany, chap. xxvi. 13. Strauss makes adroit use of this incident for his own purpose, *New Life of Jesus*, i. pp. 397–8).
[3] Luke xxiii. 56.

the core of the subject is reached. It is conceded on all hands that the Resurrection narratives present problems of exceptional interest and difficulty. It is not simply the so-called " discrepancies " in the narratives which create the problems. These, as said before, may prove to be of minor account. What are they all compared with the tremendous agreement in the testimony which Strauss himself thus formulates · " According to all the Gospels, Jesus, after having been buried on the Friday evening, and lain during the Sabbath in the grave, came out of it restored to life at day-break on Sunday " ? [1] The problems arise from the fact that now, in the historical inquiry, an unequivocal step is taken into the region of the supernatural. Naturalism or supernaturalism—there is no escape from the alternative presented. There are consequently two, and only two, possible avenues of approach to these narratives, and according as the one or the other is adopted, the light in which they appear will be different. If they are approached, as they are by most " moderns," with the fixed persuasion that there is, and can be, no resurrection of the dead, it is impossible to avoid seeing in them only a farrago of contradictions and incredibilities. For it is undeniably a supernatural fact which they record—the revivification of the Son of God, the supreme act of triumph

[1] *New Life of Jesus*, i. p. 397.

by which the Redeemer of the world, through the might of the Father, resumed the life He had voluntarily laid down.[1] The element in which they move is the supernatural—the earthquake which opens a path from the tomb and scatters the guards ; angelic appearances and messages ; manifestations of the Risen Lord Himself. If nothing of this can be accepted, the narratives, with the faith which they embody, and the effects of that faith in history, remain an enigma, incapable, as the attempts at the reading of their riddle show, of solution.[2]

Here, then, a choice must be made. If Strauss's dictum, " Every historian should possess philosophy enough to be able to deny miracles here as well as elsewhere,"[3] is accepted, it becomes an insult to intelligence to speak of the narratives as evidence of anything. If, on the other hand, with scope for the discussion of details, the presence of the supernatural in the heart of the narratives is frankly acknowledged, harmony speedily begins to manifest itself where before there was irreconcilable confusion. As R. H. Hutton, a man of no

[1] John x. 17, 18 ; cf. Matt. xx. 28, etc.

[2] Justly has Prof. F. Loofs said : " He who has never felt that, with the message, 'Christ is risen,' something quite extraordinary, all but incomprehensible to natural experience, has entered into the history of the world, has not yet rightly understood what it is to preach the Risen One " (*Die Auferstehungsberichte*, p. 7).

[3] Quoted by Godet, *Com. on St. John*, iii. p. 323.

narrow intellect and a cultured judge of historical evidence, puts it : " The whole incredibility which has been felt in relation to this statement [the Lord's Resurrection] arises, I imagine, entirely from its supernatural and miraculous character. . . . A short statement of how the matter really stands will prove, I think, that, were the fact *not* supernatural, the various inconsistencies in the evidence adduced of it would not weigh a jot with any reasonable mind against accepting it." [1]

It is in this spirit that the discussion of the Resurrection narratives will be approached in the succeeding chapters. The evidence will be taken as it is given—not with the *à priori* demand for some other kind of evidence, but with the aim of ascertaining the value of that actually possessed. It will be fully recognized that, as before allowed, the narratives are fragmentary, condensed, often generalized,[2] are different in points of view, difficult in

---

[1] *Theol. Essays*, third edition, p. 131. The whole essay should be consulted.

[2] In illustration of what is meant by " generalizing," the following may be adapted from Ebrard (*Gospel History*, pp. 450–1). A friend is at the point of death. On returning from a journey, I am ,met in succession by different persons, one of whom tells me of his illness, two others inform me of his death, while a fourth gives me a parting message. In writing later to an acquaintance, I state briefly that on my way home I had met four friends, who had given me the particulars of his illness and death, and conveyed to me his last dying words. Of what interest would it be to the recipient of the letter to know whether

some respects to fit into each other, yet generally, with patient inspection, furnishing a key to the solution of their own difficulties—receiving also no small elucidation from the better-ordered story of St. John. In contrast with the extraordinary treatment accorded to them by the newer school, the study, it is hoped, will do something to create or strengthen confidence in their credibility.

all the friends came together, or separately, which came first and which brought the message ? In the same way, it mattered little to the readers of the Synoptic Gospels to know whether the women all went together to the grave, or whether one went before the rest, etc. Yet in this lies most of the difficulty.

CREDIBILITY *conti*

V

CREDIBILITY *continued*—" THE EASTER MESSAGE "

PROFESSOR HARNACK, in his lectures on Christianity, bids us hold by " the Easter faith " that " Jesus Christ has passed through death, that God has awakened Him to life and glory," but warns us against basing this faith on " the Easter message of the empty grave, and the appearances of Jesus to His disciples." [1] On what, then, one asks, is the faith to be based which connects it peculiarly with Easter ? Or on what did the Apostles and the whole primitive Church base it, except on their conviction that, in St. Paul's words,[2] Jesus " was buried, and that He hath been raised on the third day according to the Scriptures ; and that He appeared to Cephas," and to the others named ? But in all these " stories told by Paul and the Evangelists," Professor Harnack reminds us, " there is no tradition of single events which is quite trustworthy." [3]

[1] *What is Christianity ?* pp. 160–3.
[2] 1 Cor. xv. 4–6.   [3] P. 162.

It is this assertion of the insecurity of the Easter message of the Resurrection as a basis for faith which is now to be tested. Attention will be given first to the points which are more central and essential. It is, of course, easy to spirit away every part of the evidence by sufficiently bold denials, and by constructions which betray their weakness in the fact that hardly two of them agree together. It will be seen as the inquiry proceeds that the contradictions imputed to the Evangelists are trifles compared with those of the critics among themselves in seeking to amend the history. Agreeing only in rejecting the evidence of the Gospels as to what actually happened, they lose themselves in a maze of contradictory conjectures.

A few examples may be of service.

Weizsäcker, like Pfleiderer, is certain that St. Paul knew nothing of the women's visit to the grave. "The only possible explanation," he says, "is that the Apostle was ignorant of its existence."[1] "Paul," says Pfleiderer, "knows nothing of the women's discovery of the empty grave."[2] Professor Lake, on the other hand, thinks that St. Paul *did* know of it, and accounts in this way for his mention of "the third day."[3]

Further, as "Paul's knowledge of these things

[1] *Apost. Age*, E. T., i. p. 5.
[2] *Christian Origins*, p. 134.
[3] *Res. of Jesus Christ*, pp. 191–6.

must have come from the heads of the primitive Church," Weizsäcker deduces that " it is the primitive Church itself that was ignorant of any such tradition."[1] The visit of the women must there fore be dismissed as baseless legend. Keim agrees.[2] But Renan,[3] Réville, H. J. Holtzmann,[4] O. Holtzmann, Professor Lake—indeed most—accept the fact as historical.

Another crucial point is the empty tomb. Strauss, Keim, and, more recently, A. Meyer [5] treat the empty grave as an inference from belief in the Resurrection. But a " hundred voices," Keim acknowledges, are raised in protest, and " many critics, not only of the Right, but even of the Left, are able to regard it [the empty grave] as certain and incontrovertible."[6] " There is no reason to doubt," says O. Holtzmann, " that the women did not carry out their intention of anointing, because they found the grave empty."[7] Renan does not dream of questioning the fact.

Many critics, including Professor Lake,[8] think it impossible that Jesus should have spoken of His death and Resurrection on the third day. Others, as A. Meyer [9] and O. Holtzmann,[10] find in such say-

---

[1] *Ut supra.*   [2] *Jesus of Nazara*, E. T., vi. p. 296.
[3] *Les Apôtres*, ch. i.   [4] *Die Synoptiker*, p. 105.
[5] *Die Auferstehung Christi*, pp. 120–25.
[6] *Ut supra*, pp. 297–8.   [7] *Leben Jesu*, p. 391.
[8] *Ut supra*, pp. 255–9.
[9] *Ut supra*, pp. 181–2.   [10] *Ut supra*, p. 388.

ings of Jesus an important element in the development of belief in the Resurrection.

A favourite view, shared by Strauss, Weizsäcker, Keim, Pfleiderer, A. Meyer, Professor Lake, is that the disciples, immediately after the Crucifixion, fled to Galilee, there, and not at Jerusalem, receiving the visions which convinced them that the Lord had risen.[1]   On this hypothesis, the women, even if they visited the tomb, had no share in the origin of the belief in the Resurrection.[2]   Most, on the other hand, who, like Renan [3] and H. J. Holtzmann,[4] accept the visit to the tomb, hold that the Apostles were still in Jerusalem on the Easter morning.

To return to the positive investigation.   It has already been seen that no doubt can rest on the cardinal fact that Jesus *did* die, and was buried ; and Harnack will allow a connexion of the Easter message with " that wonderful event in Joseph of Arimathæa's Garden," which, however, he says, " no eye saw." [5]   What was the nature of that connexion ?

I. It is the uncontradicted testimony of all the witnesses that it *was* the *Easter morning,* or, as the Evangelists call it, " the first day of the week,"

---

[1] Weizsäcker, i. pp. 2, 3 ; Keim, vi. pp. 281 ff. ; A. Meyer, pp. 121, 127–30, etc.
[2] A Meyer, p. 124 ; Lake, p. 195.
[3] *Les Apôtres*, ch. i.
[4] *Ut supra*, p. 105.   [5] *Ut supra*, p. 161.

or *third day* after the Crucifixion, on which the
event known as the Resurrection happened ; in
other words, that Jesus rose from the dead *on the
third day.* The four Evangelists, whatever their
other divergences, are agreed about this.[1] The
Apostle Paul, who had conversed with the original
witnesses only eight or nine years after the event,[2]
confirms the statement, and declares it to be the
general belief of the Church.[3] Not a ripple of
dubiety can be shown to rest on the belief. " There
is no doubt," Professor Lake allows, " that from
the beginning the Resurrection was believed to
have taken place on the third day.[4]

Here, then, it might seem, is an unchallengeable
basis from which to start, for a whole Christian
Church can hardly be conceived of as mistaken
about an elementary fact connected with its own
origin. But the fact is not unchallenged. Nothing in this history is. Strauss long ago set the
example in endeavouring to show how the belief
might have originated from Old Testament hints.[5]

---

[1] Matthew xxviii. 1 ; Mark xvi. 2 ; Luke xxiv. 1 ;
John xx. 1. The predictions of Jesus of His rising on the
third day may be added, if only as evidence of the belief.

[2] Galatians i. 18, 19 ; ii. 1, 9. Strauss says " There is
no occasion to doubt that the Apostle Paul had heard this
from Peter, James, and others concerned." (*New Life
of Jesus,* i. p. 400.)

[3] 1 Corinthians xv. 3.

[4] *Ut supra,* p. 253 ; cf. p. 264.

[5] *Ut supra,* i. pp. 438-9.

Professor Lake, who thinks it rests " on theological rather than historical grounds,"[1] devotes some twenty-five pages of his book, in different places, to weaken its foundations.[2] A new Babylonian school derives it from pagan myths.[3] A writer like A. Meyer combines all the standpoints, and would explain it from Old Testament passages, predictions of Jesus, and Greek, Persian, and Babylonian analogies.[4]

It is difficult to know what to make of a criticism of this kind, which so boldly sets aside existing evidence to launch out on assertions for which no proof can be given. It is the more difficult in Professor Lake's case, that in the end he accepts the Marcan tradition of the visit of the women to the tomb—or what they took to be the tomb—on the morning of the third day after the Crucifixion, for the purpose of anointing.[5] If they did—and who can reasonably doubt it ?—why all this pother in seeking an explanation from Old Testament suggestions, Babylonian mythology, and other obscure quarters ? It is argued, to be sure, that even the experience of the women was not a proof that the Resurrection did not take place on the

---

[1] *Ut supra*, p. 264.
[2] Cf. pp. 27–33, 191–3, 196–9, 253–65.
[3] Cf. Cheyne, *Bible Problems*, pp. 110 ff. ; Lake, pp. 197–8, 261.
[4] *Ut supra*, pp. 178–85.
[5] *Ut supra*, pp. 182, 196, 246, etc.

second day rather than on the *third*, and mythology is called in to help to fix the day.[1] One reads
even : " It is never stated, but only implied in
Mark that the Resurrection was on the third day." [2]
As if, in St. Mark's time, a single soul in the Church
had a doubt on that subject !

The treatment of St. Paul's testimony to " the
third day " is not less arbitrary. The attempt is
made by Professor Lake to separate St. Paul's
mention of the third day from his witness to the
appearances ; " the strongest evidence for the alternative [negative] view " being, that it requires
that St. Paul should have said, " and was seen
on the third day," not " and was raised on the third
day." [3] One asks, Could Jesus have been seen
until He was raised ? It is granted that St. Paul
was acquainted with the Jerusalem tradition which
embraced this fact.[4] Yet several pages discuss,
with indecisive result, whether " the third day "
was not " merely a deduction from Scripture." [5]
The conclusion is that, whatever St. Paul's reason
(it is allowed later on that it is " not impossible "
that his reference may be to the experience of the
women),[6] " we can only be almost certain that it
cannot have been anything which he was able to
rank as first-hand evidence of the Resurrection." [7]

[1] Pp. 254, 259–63.   [2] P. 198.   [3] Pp. 27–8.
[4] P. 41.   [5] Pp. 29–32.   [6] P. 196.
     [7] P. 32.

Is not the unreality of such reasoning itself a powerful corroboration of the historicity of the Gospel and Pauline statements?

2. The next important element in the witness, in part implied in the preceding, is *the visit of the women to the tomb of Jesus* at early morning on the third day.[1] Here, again, with some variation, we have a substantial nucleus of agreement. The differences will be looked at immediately; but how little they touch the main matter is apparent from the circumstance that, even among the extremer sceptics, the greater number admit that the women—the same named in the Gospels—*did* go to visit the tomb of Jesus on that memorable morning. Strauss can hardly admit it, for he throws doubt on the previous fact of the burial. But most who allow that Jesus was laid in the (or *a*) rock-tomb admit that the sorrowing women who had followed Him from Galilee, and had witnessed the Crucifixion and entombment,[2] or members of their company, did, as was most natural, come to the tomb on the morning after the close of the Sabbath, as day was breaking, for the purpose of anointing the body. Professor Lake admits this; the two Holtzmanns admit it; even

---

[1] Matthew xxviii. 1; Mark xvi. 1, 2; Luke xxiv. 1, 10; cf. xxiii. 55; John xx. 1.

[2] Cf. Matthew xxvii. 55, 56; Mark xv. 40, 41; Luke xxiii. 49; John xix. 25.

A. Meyer, although, without the least ground, he disconnects the incident from the third day, concedes that visits were made.[1] Renan gives a summary of the facts, yet with a touch of inconsistency with his previous statements which, in the Evangelists, would be called " contradiction," he tells, e.g., of " the Galilean women who on the Friday evening had hastily embalmed the body," [2] forgetful that earlier he had correctly described the embalming as performed by Joseph and Nicodemus.[3]

The essential point being thus conceded, long time need not be spent on the alleged discrepancies with regard to (i) the *names and number* of the women. St. John's account in this connexion will be considered by itself. Meanwhile what must strike every careful reader is, that the names of all, or most, of the women concerned are, if not directly in the narratives of the Resurrection, yet in the related accounts of the closing scenes, given by each of the Evangelists. It is St. Mark, the supposed source, that tells how, at the Crucifixion, " there were also women beholding from afar : among whom were both Mary Magdalene, and Mary the mother of James the less, and of Joses, and Salome, who, when He was in Galilee, followed Him and ministered unto Him ; and many

---

[1] *Ut supra*, p. 124. His account is referred to below.
[2] *Les Apôtres*, p. 6.   [3] *Vie de Jésus*, p. 431.

other women which came up with Him to Jerusalem "; [1] and how, at the burial, " Mary Magdalene and Mary the mother of Joses beheld where
He was laid." [2]   These two, with Salome, are then
described as buying spices and coming to the tomb
on the Resurrection morning.[3]   St. Matthew gives
the like story of " many women beholding from
afar, which had followed Jesus from Galilee,"
" among whom was Mary Magdalene, and Mary
the mother of James and Joses, and the mother of
the sons of Zebedee (Salome)," [4] and tells, as before,
of Mary Magdalene and the other Mary " sitting
over against the sepulchre." [5]   It is extravagant
to suppose that because St. Matthew, following
up this statement, speaks of " Mary Magdalene
and the other Mary " [6] coming to the sepulchre
on the first day of the week, and omits the mention of Salome, he designs to contradict St. Mark,
who includes her. [7] St. Luke, likewise, knows of
" the women that followed with Him from Galilee," [8] and who (therefore not the two Marys only)
beheld where He was laid,[9] and came with their

---

[1] Mark xv. 40.   [2] Ver. 47.
[3] Mark xvi. 1.   [4] Matt. xxvii. 55, 56.
[5] Ver. 61.   [6] Matthew xxviii. 10.
[7] It would be as reasonable to accuse St. Mark of contradiction because in one verse he speaks of " Mary the
mother of James the less and of Joses," and in another
of " Mary the mother of Joses " only.
[8] Luke xxiii. 49.   [9] Ver. 55.

spices on the first-day morning.[1] St. Luke gives the list afterwards as " Mary Magdalene, and Joanna, and Mary the mother of James, and the other women with them." (Salome is omitted and Joanna the wife of Chuza, Herod's steward, appears.[2]) St. John corroborates the others in speaking of Christ's " mother and His mother's sister [probably Salome, so Meyer, Alford, etc.], Mary the wife of Clopas and Mary Magdalene," [3] at the Cross ; but at the Resurrection he speaks only of Mary Magdalene,[4] of whom he has a special story to tell. The " we," however, in St. John xx. 2, implies the presence of others.

Is there really any difficulty of moment in these various narratives ? They are incomplete, but surely they are not contradictory. The same group of women is in the background in each ; Mary Magdalene and " the other Mary," are the prominent figures in all : the mention of other names is determined by the preference or special object of the Evangelist. It is most natural that the mourning women should repair at the earliest moment on the morning after the Sabbath to the tomb of their crucified Master, to " see " it, as St. Matthew says,[5] and, if access could be obtained, to complete the rites of burial. There is no need for supposing that they came together ; it is much

[1] Luke xxiv. 1. [2] Ver. 10. [3] John xix. 25.
[4] John xx. i. [5] Matthew xxviii. 1.

more probable that they came in different groups or companies—perhaps Mary Magdalene and the other Mary, or these with Salome, first, to be joined after by Joanna and other members of the Galilean band.[1] Nothing, as was before noted, can be inferred from St. Matthew omitting to mention the design of anointing. His story of the guard, as rendering the anointing impossible, may have influenced him : only that the women knew nothing of the guard. It is not that the Evangelist was ignorant of the custom of anointing ;[2] but, following up the picture he had drawn of the two Marys " sitting over against " the sepulchre at the burial,[3] he gives prominence to the yearning of love these women felt to see again where the Lord slept.[4]

There remains (ii) the *time* of this visit of the women, as to which, again, discrepancy is frequently alleged. Certain of the notes of time in the Evangelists raise interesting exegetical questions (e.g., St. Matthew's " late on the Sabbath

[1] After enumerating the women Renan says : " They came, probably each on her own account, for it is difficult to call in question the tradition of the three Synoptical Gospels, according to which several women came to the tomb : on the other hand, it is certain that in the two most authentic narratives [?] which we possess of the Resurrection, Mary Magdalene alone played a part." (*Les Apôtres*, p. 6.)

[2] Cf. Matthew xxvi. 12.   [3] Matthew xxvii. 61.

[4] Matthew xxviii. 1.

day " ; [1] St. Mark's " when the sun was risen " [2]) ;
but real contradiction it is hard to discover. What
can be readily observed is that no one of the Evangelists employs the precise expression of another
—a strong proof of independence ; [3] and further,
that all the expressions imply that the visits took
place at, or about, early dawn, or daybreak, when
darkness was passing into day. St. Matthew
gives the description, " late on the Sabbath day "
(ὀψὲ δὲ σαββάτων), as it began to dawn (τῇ ἐπιφωσ-
κούσῃ) towards the first day of the week." [4] St. Mark
says : " Very early (λίαν πρωΐ) on the first day
of the week   when the sun was risen " (ἀνατεί-
λαντος τοῦ ἡλίου).[5] St. Luke has the expression :
" At early dawn " (ὄρθρου βαθέος) [6] St. John
has : " Early (πρωΐ), while it was yet dark." [7]
The discrepancies between these expressions are
formal only. If contradiction there is, it lies chiefly
in St. Mark's own apparently inconsistent clauses,
" very early," and " when the sun was risen." [8]

[1] Matthew xxviii. 1.   [2] Mark xvi. 2.
[3] Alford wrote : " The independence and distinctness
of the four narratives in this part have never been questioned " (on Matt. xxviii. 1). This, too, needs qualifying.
[4] Matthew xxviii. 1. Meyer observes : " Consequently
the point of time mentioned here is substantially identical
with that given in Luke xxiv. 1, and in John xx. i " (in
loc.).
[5] Mark xvi. 2.   [6] Luke xxiv. 1.   [7] John xx. 1.
[8] Scholars are well agreed that the aorist participle here
can only bear the sense : " After the sun was risen."

As the Evangelist cannot be supposed to intend
verbally to contradict himself within the compass
of one verse, his language must reasonably be construed to mean : " At early dawn, when the sun was
just above the horizon." Similarly, St. Matthew's
" late on the Sabbath day " cannot reasonably be put into contradiction with his own ex-
planatory clause · " As it began to dawn towards
the first day of the week." It is not, as the con
text shows,[1] Saturday night that is meant, but
the period of darkness ending at dawn of the fol
lowing morning (thus Meyer, Alford, etc.). The
view advocated by some that St. Matthew, borrowing from St. Mark, here combines inconsistent
clauses by dropping out St. Mark's mention of the
purchase of spices between,[2] is, as Meyer remarks, •
untenable. It is not St. Mark's language that
is used, and St. Matthew may be credited with

---

[1] Some, as McClellan, *The New Testament*, pp. 512–31,
insist that St. Matthew's " late on the Sabbath " can only
mean Saturday evening, and explain the subsequent clause
by the help of Luke xxiii. 54, " And the Sabbath drew
on " (ἐπέφωσκε). But the events that follow in St. Matthew plainly belong to the morning of the first day. Mc-
Clellan acknowledges that " nearly every modern writer
of importance [a long list] interprets St. Matthew's phrases
as of Sunday morning."

[2] Thus Lake, p. 57 ; W. C. Allen, *St. Matthew*, pp. 300–1,
etc. : so, too, Caspari (*Chron. Introd.*, E. T., p. 240). Allen
says : " Matthew, by omitting Mark's reference to the
purchase of perfumes, has combined two entirely inconsistent notes of time." But see Meyer, *in loo.*

sufficient knowledge of Greek to keep him from
perpetrating so obvious a blunder. St. John's
" while it was yet dark " presents no difficulty
when the situation is recalled. The women began
to arrive just as day was breaking, and it was daylight before they left the place. Mary Magdalene
had light enough to see that the stone was taken
away.[1]

3. The third crucial fact in the history—one
which, in connexion with succeeding incidents,
establishes the reality of the Resurrection, is that,
when the women reached the tomb of Jesus on that
Easter morning, after much dubiety as to how
they were to obtain entrance, they found *the stone
rolled away and the tomb empty*. Here, again, there
is entire unanimity among the witnesses.[2] St.
Matthew alone tells of *how* the stone was removed
—of " a great earthquake," and the descent of an
angel of the Lord, who rolled away the stone, and
sat upon it, before whose dazzling aspect the keepers
became as dead men.[3] But all the Evangelists
agree that the stone, the rolling away of which had
caused the women much concern (" who shall roll
us away the stone from the door of the tomb ? ")[4]

[1] John xx. 1 : " Twilight in that latitude does not last
for more than a quarter of an hour " (Latham, *The Risen
Master*, p. 225).
[2] Matthew xxviii. 2–7 ; Mark xvi. 3–6 ; Luke xxiv.
2–6 ; John xx. 1, 11, 12.
[3] Matthew xxviii. 2–4.   [4] Mark xvi. 3.

was found rolled away, and that the tomb was empty, when the women arrived. In St. Mark's words · " An'd looking up, they see that the stone is rolled back ; for it was exceeding great." [1]   Or in St. Luke's : " And they found the stone rolled away from the tomb.   And they entered in, and found not the body of the Lord Jesus." [2]   According to St. John, the emptiness of the tomb was subsequently verified by St. Peter and St. John himself.[3]   Moreover, while St. Matthew alone gives the story of the rolling away of the stone by the angel, the implication in all the other narratives is that the stone was removed by supernatural power.   No human hand had effected this wonder. St. Matthew, therefore, only narrates in objective fashion—a reflection, possibly, of the terrified imagination of some of the guards—what the other Evangelists postulate.   What really had happened the women were soon to learn from angelic announcements to themselves.   Jesus had risen, as He said.[4]

Here, then, are two facts in the history of the Resurrection—*the stone rolled away*, and *the empty tomb*—attested about as well as facts can be, with the belief of the whole primitive Church behind them.   There is not a hint anywhere that the fact

---

[1] Verse 4   [2] Luke xxiv. 2, 3.
[3] John xx. 3–9 ; cf. Luke xxiv. 12.
[4] Matthew xxviii. 6.

of the empty tomb was ever questioned by either friend or foe. If would have been easy to question or disprove it when the Apostles were boldly proclaim-ing the Resurrection in Jerusalem a few weeks later.[1] But no one appears to have done so. The other fact of the rolling away of the stone with which the tomb had been closed is involved in the tomb being found empty. Taken as they stand —much more when taken in connexion with what succeeds—the two facts support belief in the Re-surrection. What is to be said of them ?

There are here only two courses if the Resurrec-tion is disputed. Either (1) the facts may be denied, and the evidence set aside, as when it is argued that the empty tomb is itself an inference from belief in the Resurrection.[2] Or (2) the facts may be admitted, and a " natural " explanation be sought for them. The extremer view has al-ready been alluded to, and need not longer detain us. It is interesting only for its implied admission that the belief of the Apostolic Church was belief in a bodily Rising. Undoubtedly every believer in the Resurrection of Christ, St. Paul included, held as part of that belief that the tomb of Jesus was left empty. But the emptiness of the tomb was not a deduction from prior belief in the Re-

[1] Acts ii. 24, 31 ; iii. 15 ; iv. 10, etc.
[2] Thus Strauss, Weizsäcker, Keim, etc.

surrection—the Apostles were guilty of no such
hysteron proteron—but was a fact by itself, adequately attested, and one of the grounds of belief
in that divine occurrence. In recent times, accordingly, the other alternative is that more commonly
adopted. It is becoming usual to accept the fact
of the empty tomb, and to seek for it, since the
Resurrection is not admitted, some natural explanation. The study of these explanations is extremely
instructive. Dr. Rashdall is quoted by Professor
Lake as saying that " were the testimony fifty
times stronger than it is, any hypothesis would
be more possible than that " of a physical resuscitation.[1] Only in the light of these " more possible "
explanations is the strength of the evidence for the
Resurrection of Jesus fully disclosed.

If the tomb was empty on the morning of that
third day, and Jesus did not rise, some other hands
must secretly have removed the body. Who did
it ? The old theory of fraud on the part of the
disciples[2] has now no respectable advocates, and
may be put out of account. Who, then, effected
the removal ? Pilate ? The Sanhedrim—the enemies of Jesus ? This has been actually defended,[3]

[1] Lake, *ut supra*, p. 269.
[2] Reimarus and some of the Deists. The calumny
noted in Matthew xxviii 12-15, is an additional proof
that the tomb was found empty.
[3] E.g., by A. Réville, Schwartzkopff, etc.: cf. A. Meyer,
ut supra, pp. 17-18.

but may also be passed over.[1]   But glance at more recent solutions.

O. Holtzmann gives the following account. The honourable councillor, Joseph of Arimathæa, having first, as the Gospels relate, permitted the burial of Jesus in his rock-tomb, felt on reflection that it would not do to havé the body of a man who had been crucified lying among the dead in his respectable family vault. He, therefore, when the Sabbath was past, had the body of Jesus secretly removed, and buried elsewhere. Such, this author thinks, is " the simplest explanation of the mysterious occurrence."[2] It is implied, of course, that the secret was carefully kept from the disciples, who were allowed to believe that their Master had risen. This interesting little deception of Joseph, so likely in a good man, and first brought to light in these last years, successfully took in the whole Christian Church, and, combined with imaginary appearances, created its faith in the Resurrection !

So transparent a piece of trickery does not appeal to Professor Lake, who gives a solution on different lines. The facts, he thinks, were probably these.

---

[1] Renan admits the empty tomb, but judiciously refrains from explanations. Cf. Latham, *The Risen Master*, pp. 6–9.

[2] *Leben Jesu*, pp. 392–3. The germ of the theory is found in H. J. Holtzmann, *Die Synoptiker*, p. 105. Cf. the criticism in A. Meyer, pp. 118–19.

The women came in the dusk of morning to an empty tomb, which they mistakenly took to be that of Jesus. The neighbourhood of Jerusalem was full of rock-tombs, and it was easy to go wrong. A young man, standing near, tried to convince them of their error, and pointed them to where the Lord really lay. [This is the young man, as previously seen, whom legend, according to Professor Lake, transforms into an angel, and also into the Risen Lord.] But the women fled. Professor Lake's own words deserve to be quoted : " The women came in the early morning to a tomb which they thought was the one in which they had seen the Lord buried. They expected to find a closed tomb, but they found an open one ; and a young man, who was in the entrance, guessing their errand, tried to tell them that they had made a mistake in the place. ' He is not here,' said he ; ' see the place where they laid Him,' and probably pointed to the next tomb. But the women were frightened at the detection of their error, and fled, only imperfectly or not at all understanding what they heard. If was only later on, when they knew that the Lord had risen [from visions of the disciples in Galilee], and—on their view—that His tomb must be empty, that they came to believe that the young man was something more than they had seen ; that he was not telling them of their mistake, but announcing the Resurrection, and that his intention was to give them a message for the disciples." [1]

As a " natural " explanation, this fairly rivals Paulus. But will any one believe that such a mistake of a few women is really the foundation on which the Christian Church has built its Easter hope, or affords an adequate explanation of the revolutionary effects in the faith and hope of the disciples which, according to all the narratives, were wrought by the experiences of that Easter morning ? If so, he has a strange idea of the relation of causes and effects. The theory, it need hardly be pointed out, is itself an invention, without historical support or probability—a travesty of the narratives as we have them. There is no evidence of a mistake of the women, who knew too well where the Lord was laid ; [2] or of the presence of the obliging young man, weeks after identified with an angel *within* the tomb ; or of a mistake of the import of the message. Were the women the only persons who visited the spot ? Did no one think of verifying their tale ? Did they never themselves go back and discover their error ? Whence this consentient and mistaken conviction that the tomb was found empty on the third day, and that a message came from it that the Lord had risen ? As a " more possible " hypothesis Professor Lake's theory may safely be set aside.

[1] *Ut supra*, pp. 251–2.
[2] Mark xv. 47 ; Luke xxiii. 55.

A last example is taken from A. Meyer, who, in his book *Die Auferstehung Christi*, after criticizing and rejecting previous theories, gives what he conjectures may be the true version of events. The passage is an excellent example of the process of manufacturing history out of moonshine. He says : " If one seeks for an historical kernel behind the narrative of Mark, it is not difficult to picture to oneself how, perhaps, after some time [indefinite], in the early morning, veiled women, disciples of Jesus, crept forth, sad and despairing, to seek the tomb and the body ; how they, perchance, had inquired about the place, how they stood some time helpless before a huge stone, and said, ' Oh, if only some one would roll away that stone for us ' ; then again in doubt before an empty cave, not knowing whether the Lord might have lain there, and some one have taken Him away ; how they may have often repeated such search, until at last the news and summons came from Galilee, ' Why seek ye the living among the dead ? He is not there, give up your seeking : He is long ago risen and has appeared to Simon and the others ; come and hear it for yourselves.' " [1]   It has only to be said of this flight of fancy that, when compared with the narrative of the Gospels, it has no substance or feature of reality in it.   It contradicts the tradition at every point.   There is no " historical

[1] P. 124.

kernel," for the ground of history is abandoned for imagination. The visit of the women is cut away from the third day : is unhistorically represented as repeated and resultless ; the message which came from the tomb is brought weeks later from Galilee, etc. Opposed to the Gospels, it is opposed equally to the theories already adduced. Unbelief here also lacks unity in its hypotheses. It shatters itself against the moveless rock of the facts.

4. And now the Easter history reaches its climax. The facts already reviewed—the third day, the visit of the women, the stone supernaturally removed, the empty tomb—lead up to, and find their natural culmination in, *the angelic vision and message that the Lord had risen.*[1] Here once more it is permissible to speak of at least essential agreement in the narratives. Particulars and phraseology in the accounts vary, as before, in a manner incompatible with dependence. St. Luke, e.g., speaks of two angels where St. Matthew and St. Mark mention only one ; and in the part of the angel's message relating to Galilee St. Luke gives the words a quite different turn from what they have in the other Gospels.[2] St. John's account stands again by itself. Yet all the Synoptical

[1] Matthew xxviii. 5–8 ; Mark xvi. 6–8 ; Luke xxiv. 4–11 ; John xx. 1, 11–12.

[2] Luke xxiv. 6, 7 ; cf. Matthew xxviii. 7 ; Mark xvi. 7.

narratives agree that, while the women stood, perplexed and affrighted at or within the tomb, they received a vision of angels ; that the announcement was made to them that the Lord had risen ; that they were invited to see the place where He had lain ; that they had given them a message to take to the disciples. In the central part of the message : " He is not here ; He is risen," there is *verbal* agreement : only St. Matthew and St. Luke reverse the order of the clauses. St. Mark breaks off with the women fleeing from the tomb in " trembling and astonishment " ;[1] but there can be no reasonable doubt that his Gospel also, not less than the others, contemplated a report of the angelic message to the disciples, and a narrative of certain of the appearances.[2] According to St. Matthew and St. Luke, the report was made on the same day.[3] The Apostles were, therefore, still in Jerusalem, and the fiction of their having already dispersed to Galilee is proved to be baseless.

The Lord had risen ! There were no witnesses of that august event ; but the fact was made certain to the faith of the disciples by the empty grave, by the angelic vision, and by the subsequent appearances of Jesus Himself. The time of the Resurrection is not told, but it is implied that it syn-

---

[1] Mark xvi. 8.
[2] Cf. the remarks in Menzies, *The Earliest Gospel*, p. 120.
[3] Matthew xxviii. 3 ; Luke xxiv. 9–11, 22, 23.

chronized with the convulsion of nature which
St. Matthew describes, and with the rolling away
of the stone by the angel which terrified and pros-
trated the guards. It therefore preceded by
some time the visit of the women. There is no
need to suppose that the guards were still there
when the women arrived. It may rather be presumed that, on recovery from their terror, they
betook themselves away as speedily as they could.
Neither need the angel of St. Matthew be understood to be still sitting on the stone as at the first.
His language to the women—" Come, see the place
where the Lord lay "—rather implies that, as in
other Gospels, he addresses them from *within* the
tomb.

It is not to be gainsaid that we have here a story
of supernatural events. The narratives are steeped
in the supernatural. The supernatural element
may be resisted, but it must at least be conceded
that the account goes together on its own assumption that a tremendous miracle—the Resurrection
of the Lord—really took place. It was before
remarked that in all the Gospels there is the implication of supernatural power in the removal
of the stone. A physical convulsion was the natural
accompaniment of so great a marvel.[1] The ap-

[1] Cf. the darkness, earthquake, and rending of the
Temple veil at the Crucifixion. Matthew xxvii. 15, 51 ;
Mark xv. 33, 37 ; Luke xxiii. 44, 45.

pearance of the angel is in keeping with what is told of the later appearances of the angels to the women. The reality of the angelic appearances, again, is vouched for by the message which, according to all the witnesses, the women received, and which they subsequently conveyed to the disciples. That message is the kernel of the whole story. It is the " Easter message " which has changed the face of the world. If anything stands fast in the Resurrection history, it is that this message did not spring from their own sad, despairing hearts, but was given them by celestial visitants at the tomb.

So closely, in truth, is this message which the women received bound up with the " vision of angels," [1] that it is difficult to see how the one is to be believed, if the other is rejected.[2] The difference in the accounts of the vision, though Strauss and later sceptics have made much of them, are not of a nature to occasion serious difficulty. There may really have been two angels, as in the experience of Mary Magdalene,[3] though only one is mentioned by St. Matthew and St. Mark : or St. Luke, in his summary narrative, may be combining the

[1] Luke xxiv. 23.

[2] There seems to the present writer no incredibility in the supposition of a higher spiritual world capable of manifesting itself, but much to favour the idea. Whatever the theory of Christ's knowledge, this is precisely one of the things on which His intuition might be trusted.

[3] John xx. 12.

experience of Mary Magdalene with that of the other women. But there is a further consideration suggested by the nature of vision itself. Whether or not it is right to speak of "ecstasy" in such an experience, it is certain that the state of "vision" (ὀπτασία) is not simply an extension of ordinary perception. It is not a state of pure objectivity. It is not on the outer but on the inner senses that an impression is made in the apprehension of the supersensible. There is, in Old Testament phrase, an "opening of the eyes,"[1] a raising of consciousness to a higher plane. What is seen is real, but there is a subjective element in the seeing. It follows that in a vision like that of the women at the tomb the experience of one is not necessarily the measure of the experience of another. When notes were compared, all would not be found to have had exactly ·the same perceptions. Especially would this be the case if there were different companies, or if the experiences registered were not those of the same moment. Yet in the main the perceptions *did* agree. Forms of men ("a young man," Mark; "two men," Luke) ;[2] "appearance like lightning, and raiment

[1] Cf. *Numbers* xxiv. 3, 16; 2 Kings vi. 17, etc.

[2] Mr. Latham's idea that the "visitants to the tomb" (and at the Ascension) may have been persons (Essenes ?) from Jerusalem (*Risen Master*, pp. 412–19), is a strange aberration. The rationalistic theory that the women may have been deceived by the glint of the grave clothes is left unnoticed.

white as snow " (Matthew) ; " arrayed in white robe " (Mark) ; " in dazzling apparel " (Luke) ; " in white " (John). Above all do the narratives agree in the words of comfort : " Fear not ye : for I know that ye seek Jesus, which hath been crucified. He is not here ; for He is risen, even as He said. Come, see the place where the Lord lay " (Matthew). " Be not amazed ; ye seek Jesus the Nazarene, which hath been crucified : He is risen ; He is not here ; behold the place where they laid Him ! " (Mark). " Why seek ye the living among the dead ? He is not here, but is risen " (Luke).

From St. Mark and St. Luke [1] we learn that the women had " entered " and inspected the tomb before this wonderful experience befell them. It is not strange that, when it came, they were " amazed " (Mark) and " affrighted " (Luke), and needed the reassurance given them. The message they received for the disciples, that Jesus was going before them into Galilee, where they would see Him, with its important variation in St. Luke, will better be considered in connexion with the appearances. The events at the tomb ended with the hasty departure of the women—" with fear and great joy," says St. Matthew ; [2] " with trembling and astonishment," because of their fear, declares St. Mark,[3] saying nothing to any one, as they

[1] Mark xvi. 5 ; Luke xxiv. 5.
[2] Matthew xxviii. 8.　　　[3] Mark xvi. 8.

hasted to fulfil their commission to the disciples.
St. Mark's Gospel, at this point, on the usual view,
breaks off : not, however, before it has told us the
things it is most essential for us to know.[1]

[1] The gospel, ending at chap. xvi. 8, is manifestly incomplete. Dean Burgon unquestionably makes out a strong
case for suspense of judgment with regard to the remaining verses (9–20). (Cf. his *Last Twelve Verses of St. Mark*).
But it is safer to regard the verses as an early Appendix.
The problems which this raises must here stand over.

CREDIBILITY *continued*—THE POST-RESURRECTION APPEARANCES

VI

CREDIBILITY *continued*—THE POST-RESURRECTION APPEARANCES

IT is the testimony of all the New Testament witnesses—of the Gospels, of the Book of Acts, of St. Paul—that Jesus did appear to His disciples after His Resurrection. It was not simply the voices of angels proclaiming to the women that He had risen—not even the eloquent fact of the empty tomb—which produced in the disciples the immovable conviction that their Master had indeed burst the bands of death, and lived to die no more.[1] They believed, and unitedly testified, that they had seen Him, conversed with Him, eaten and drunk with Him ;[2] could give place, and date, and names, to His appearances to them. Often in the primitive circles, while the Apostles were still in their midst at Jerusalem, must the story of the time, occasion and manner of the chief of these manifestations, and of the incidents connected with them, have been recited.

[1] The reports of the women and of others were at first received with incredulity (Mark xvi. 11, 13, 14 ; Luke xxiv. 11).　　[2] Acts x. 41.

There is a point here, it should be noted in passing, in which the weakness of the assault on the testimony for the Resurrection is specially apparent. The assumption, practically, of the hostile critics of that testimony is that the Church had no history ; that it knew nothing, really, of its own past ; that myths and legends grew up in rank abundance, and were everywhere eagerly received ; that the writers of the Gospels had no scrupulous conscience for truth, but imagined, manipulated, and altered their materials at pleasure.[1] Any Church of our own day could give a good account of its origin, and of the events in its history, say, for the past fifty years. But the Churches founded by the Apostles —even the Mother-Church at Jerusalem—are believed to have had no such capability. The early believers had a different opinion of their knowledge and responsibility,[2] and of their ability to discern between true and false. They were not so ready as the objectors imagine to be imposed on by " cunningly devised fables." [3] The Church to which they belonged had a continuous history ; they *thought* they knew how it originated, on what facts it was based, who were its early witnesses, and to what they testified ; and they told their story without doubt or hesitation.

[1] This is really the assumption, e.g., underlying the Abbé Loisy's newly published *Les Évangiles Synoptiques.*
[2] Cf. St. Paul, 1 Cor. xv. 15.   [3] 2 Peter i. 16

This witness which the Apostles bore had nothing vague or intangible about it. It was in large part full, detailed, circumstantial. It was not "appearauces" simply, but prolonged interviews, that were alleged. The testimony must be treated in view of the actual circumstances and relations between persons in the Apostolic community— another point often overlooked. When, e.g., it is argued, as by Weizsäcker [1] that, when the author of the Acts makes St. Peter say, " We ate and drank with Him after He rose from the dead," [2] he employs a mode of representing the Risen Christ impossible to St. Paul, it has to be asked whether St. Luke, who accompanied St. Paul for so many years, would have ventured to put into the mouths of St. Peter and of St. Paul himself [3] such speeches as are found in Acts, if they had been wholly alien to the Apostles' belief and testimony.[4] We are brought here, in short, to the alternative : either narratives of the kind must be dismissed as wilful fiction, for unconscious legend is impossible in face of the knowledge which the Church possessed of its own beginnings ; or if they are allowed to rest on original authentic tradition, they can leave no doubt upon the mind that Jesus was believed to

---

[1] *Apost. Age*, i. p. 10. Thus also Loisy, ii. p. 772.
[2] Acts x. 41.   [3] E.g., Acts xiii. 31.
[4] Weizsäcker does not, of course, admit St. Luke's authorship of the Acts. His argument breaks down for every one who does.

have risen and to have appeared in bodily reality to His disciples.

The fact, however, as before, remains, and has now to be dealt with, that the narratives of the Resurrection appearances *are* challenged, and, line by line, point by point, the story which they tell is sought to be discredited. The grounds on which this is done are various. It is objected that the Gospels give different versions of these appearances, and that none gives *all* the appearances; that the evidence, even if allowed, is not of a kind to satisfy the demands of science—Renan, e.g., asks that the miracle of resurrection be performed before " a commission composed of physiologists, physicists, chemists, persons accustomed to historical criticism," and be repeated as often as desired; [1] that Jesus appeared to none but His own disciples; that legends of resurrection are not uncommon, and are explicable from natural tendencies of the mind.[2] To all which it is sufficient at present to reply that

[1] *Vie de Jésus*, Introd. pp. i., ii.

[2] " Heroes," Renan declares, " do not die." " At the moment when Mohammed expired Omar issued from the tent sabre in hand, and declared he would strike off the head of any one who would dare to say that the Prophet was no more " (*Les Apôtres*, p. 3). But heroes *do* die, and the parallel is without relevance. Mohammed's followers never seriously claimed that the Prophet did not die, or had risen from the dead. There is no instance in history, apart from Christianity, of a religion established on belief in the Resurrection of its Founder. This is discussed later. Cf. chap. viii.

the evidence was not designed to satisfy scientific experts,[1] but to produce faith in those "chosen before of God,"[2] that they might be " witnesses " to others ; and that, as observed earlier, it is not here proposed to set up *a priori* demands for evidence, but to examine carefully what evidence we have, and to ask whether, with what else is known of Jesus, it is not sufficient to sustain the faith that He is risen from the dead,˙ nay, to shut us up to that faith as the only reasonable explanation of the facts.

It' is desirable to begin in this inquiry by collecting the evidence for the appearances, and considering generally the value to be attached to the same. The several appearances can then be discussed in order.

There *were*, as already said, appearances of the Risen Jesus, or what were taken to be such, to His followers. St. Paul's list in 1 Corinthians xv. 3–8 is allowed even by the most sceptical to afford unassailable testimony on this head.[3] It is further implied in the accounts, and is generally conceded, that these appearances extended over a considerable time—at least some days or weeks.

---

[1] Cf. Luke xvi. 30, 31. A mere intellectual conviction, even if produced, would have been of no avail for the end proposed. [2] Acts x. 40–1.

[3] Strauss, *New Life of Jesus*, i. p. 400. Renan, *Les Apôtres*, p. ix. Weizsäcker, *Apost. Age*, ch. i. Keim, *Jesus of Nazara*, vi. p. 279 and generally.

St. Luke states the period at " forty days." [1]   " In Matthew," Strauss says, " the appearance of Jesus upon the mountain in Galilee must be supposed to have taken place long enough after the Resurrection to give time for the disciples to return back from Jerusalem to Galilee," [2]   St. Paul [3] and St. John likewise assume a considerable period during which Jesus was manifested to His disciples.   The chronological datum of St. Luke in Acts i. 3 must be allowed to rule the interpretation of the obviously condensed (" foreshortened ") account of the closing chapter of his Gospel.   Events, as will be seen later, were there compressed which were afterwards to be narrated more in detail.

Furthermore, the witnesses to the appearances of Jesus are *many*, and all, it can be claimed, are entitled to be heard with a presumption of their honesty and credibility.   Only leading points need be recalled.   It was before stated that St. John is here unhesitatingly accepted as an eye-witness. St. Mark was the companion of St. Peter, St. Luke was the companion of St. Paul, and a zealous investigator on his own account. [4] St. Paul had direct communication with St. Peter, St. James, St. John, and other members of the original Apostolic company. [5]

---

[1] Acts i. 3.   [2] *Ut supra*, ii. p. 420.

[3] Renan finds in 1 Cor. xv. 3–8 evidence of " the long duration of the appearances."   Cf. Acts xiii. 31.

[4] Luke i. 1–4.

[5] Gal. i. 18, 19 ; ii. 1, 9 ; Acts ix. 26 7.

St. Matthew is believed to be connected with at least the original of his Gospel—to stand in a real way behind it. The Appendix to St. Mark is yet an unsolved problem. The fact that it appears in nearly all extant MSS. and versions [1] points to a very early date, and perhaps to a close relation with St. Mark himself. It does not seem warranted to regard it as simply a summary of incidents based on St. Luke and St. John.[2] It does not show linguistic dependence on the other Gospels ; furnishes original (Mark-like) details ; bears generally a stamp of a distinct and authentic tradition.[3]

The *amplitude* and *weight* of the evidence will best

---

[1] The section (chap. xvi. 9–20) is absent, as is well known, from Cod. Sin. and Cod. Vat., from Syr. Sin., from some Armenian and Ethiopic MSS., etc. ; on the other hand, " it is supported by the vast majority of uncials," " by the cursives in a body," by all lectionaries and most versions. (Cf. art. " Mark " in Hastings' *Dict. of Bible*, iii. p. 252.) On the adverse patristic testimony, see Burgon, chap. v.

[2] Keim describes it unjustly as " a violent attempt at adjustment between Mark and Luke-John, between Galilee and Jerusalem " (vi. p. 318). The incidents in the Appendix must all have been well known in the early circles to which St. Mark (son of the Mary in whose home the Church met for worship, Acts xii. 12) belonged.

[3] Mr. Latham (*Risen Master*, pp. 202–3) is a little hard on the Appendix in fastening on its emphasis of " unbelief " (vers. 11, 16). It is precisely in St. Mark and St. Matthew that the emphasis is laid on ἀπιστία (Mark vi. 6 ; ix. 24 ; Matt. xiii. 58 ; xvii. 20), St. Luke uses the verb in chap. xxiv. 11, 41. On upbraiding, cf. Luke xxiv. 25.

be seen by a survey of its particulars as furnished by these various witnesses :—

1. St. Mark breaks off at chapter xvi. 8, but in verse 7 forecasts a meeting of Jesus with the disciples in Galilee, as Jesus had foretold.[1] This is evidently the collective meeting which St. Matthew narrates.

2. St. Matthew narrates the meeting in Galilee (on " the mountain where Jesus had appointed them "),[2] but tells also of an appearance to the women on the morning of the Resurrection. The Galilean meeting, with its great Commission, " Go ye, therefore, and make disciples of all the nations," etc., is the objective of St. Matthew's Gospel, and to it he hastens without pausing on intermediate events. Yet the fact that he relates the appearance of the women (in which that to Mary Magdalene may be merged),[3] shows that the appointed meeting was not held to exclude earlier appearances.

3. St. Luke has a rich store of original tradition, confined, however, to Jerusalem and its neighbourhood. While St. Matthew concentrates on the meeting in Galilee, St. Luke is chiefly interested in the appearances on the Resurrection day and

[1] Cf. Mark xiv. 28 ; Matt. xxvi. 32. " After I am raised up I will go before you into Galilee."

[2] Matt. xxviii. 16–20. Regarding this " appointment " the Gospels are silent. Only the promise is given : " There shall ye see Him [Me] " (Matt. xxviii. 7–10 ; Mark xvi. 7).

[3] Matt. xxviii. 9, 10. Cf. John xx. 14–17.

in Jerusalem, as leading up to the promise of the Spirit, and the Ascension at Bethany. His accounts include an appearance to St. Peter,[1] the appearance to the two disciples on the way to Emmaus,[2] an appearance to the eleven in the evening [3]—these all on Easter Day—finally, a meeting, more fully reported in Acts, on the day of Ascension.[4] Nothing is said of appearances in Galilee, though ample room is left for these, if indeed they are not implied in the " forty days " of Acts i. 3.[5]

4. St. John, writing, it is to be remembered, with knowledge of the other Gospels, gives additional valuable information concerning the events of the Resurrection morning, and records, besides the appearance to Mary Magdalene in the garden, [6] an appearance to the assembled disciples that same evening,[7] another appearance to the eleven eight days after,[8] and an appearance to seven disciples some time later, at the Lake of Galilee.[9] St. John's narratives abound in minute touches which only personal knowledge could impart.

5. St. Paul's list in 1 Corinthians xi. 3-8—the earliest written testimony, and of undoubted genuineness—covers a wide area. It leaves un-

---

[1] Luke xxiv. 34. Cf. 1 Cor. xv. 5.
[2] Luke xxv. 13, 32.   [3] Vers. 33-43.
[4] Vers. 50, 51 ; cf. Acts i. 4-12.
[5] " Appearing to them by the space of forty days " (Acts i. 3).
[6] John xx. 14-17.   [7] John xx. 19-25.
[8] Vers. 26-28.   [9] John xxi. 1-14.

noticed the appearances to the women, but enumerates an appearance to St. Peter, one to the " twelve "
(more strictly " the eleven ") [1] one to over five
hundred brethren at once, the majority of them
still living, one to St. James, and yet another to
all the Apostles. To this series St. Paul adds, as
of equal validity with the rest, the appearance to
himself.

One point about this list is of interest in connexion
with the question of " silence " in the Gospels. St.
Luke was St. Paul's companion. Apart from what
he must often have heard from St. Paul's own lips,
he was undoubtedly familiar with this Epistle to
the Corinthians, with its enumeration of appearances.
Yet in his Gospel and in Acts he omits all mention
of the great appearance to the five hundred brethren
at once (probably to be identified with St Matthew's
Galilean meeting), and of the appearance to St.
James.[2] This bears also on the point of the Evangelist's supposed ignorance in his Gospel of any longer
interval than a single day between the Resurrection
and the Ascension.[3] How, it may be asked, was

---

[1] Professor Lake says · " ' The twelve ' is the title
of a body of men who were originally twelve in number,
but it had become a conventional name, and bore no
necessary relation to the actual number " (p. 37).

[2] Cf. the remarks of Godet on this point in his *Com.
on St. Luke*, E. T., ii. p. 363.

[3] Thus Strauss, Weizsäcker, Keim, etc., but also Meyer,
Alford and others. Surely, however, it is evident of itself
that St. Luke could not suppose that the journey to Beth-

this possible, in view of the explicit testimony of St. Paul, known to St. Luke, to Christ's numerous appearances ? Acts i. makes it plain that St. Luke did know.

6. Lastly, the Appendix to St. Mark contains brief notices of *three* of the above appearances— the appearance to Mary Magdalene, that to the two disciples, and an appearance to the eleven.[1] It is probable that, as in St. Luke, this one appearance to the eleven is made to stand for all, and that some of the injunctions attached to it really belong to other meetings.

In estimating the *value* of this range of testimony, the following points are of significance. It will be seen—(1) that, while certain of the appearances depend on one witness, most are doubly or even triply attested ; (2) that, while of one or two we have only brief notices, of most there are detailed accounts ; (3) that, if the narratives are at all to be trusted, they leave no room for doubt as to the Resurrection of the Lord in the body. Special weight in this connexion must be attached to the testimony of St. John and St. Paul—one a personal witness, the other basing on first-hand communications. It is of interest, accordingly, to note how large a part of the entire case is covered by the

any and the Ascension (chap. xxiv. 50, 51) took place late at night after a crowded day, and the prolonged evening meeting detailed in vers. 39-49. See next chapter.

[1] Mark xvi. 9-20.

testimony of these two. Thus St. John attests :
(1) the appearance to Mary Magdalene, whose summons brought him to the tomb ; [1] (2) *two* appearances to the eleven, at both of which he was present ; [2]
and (3) the meeting at the Lake of Galilee, at which
again he was present [3]—*four* instances out of a total
of ten. St. Paul again attests : (1) the appearance
to St. Peter ; (2) *two* appearances to the Apostles,
one coinciding with one of St. John's ; (3) the
appearance to the five hundred ; and (4) the appearance to St. James—*four* additional to St. John's,
or, between the two, *eight* appearances. A further
noteworthy result is that, with the exception of
the appearance to the women in St. Matthew,
the *singly* attested appearances are among the *best*
attested, for they are included in the above ˙list ;
likewise the *greater* appearances, if, as is usually
assumed, the appearance to the five hundred is to
be identified with the meeting in Galilee, are, with
one exception (the appearance to the disciples on
the way to Emmaus), all included here. It will be
shown after that the Emmaus narrative, corroborated by the Appendix to St. Mark, is one of the
most credible of the series.

On the basis of this analysis, the attempt may
now be made to place the recorded appearances
in their *order*, and to exhibit the degree of attestation
that pertains to each. It is only to be borne in mind

[1] John xx. 3.　　[2] Vers. 19-29.　　[3] John xxi. 2.

what formerly was said, that in no case is it the design of the Evangelists to furnish *proofs* for the Resurrection.[1] Their object is simply to supply information, each in accordance with his particular aim, regarding a fact already universally believed. Each gives his own selection of incidents, and no single narrative makes any pretence to be complete.[2]

The appearances to the disciples may be arranged as follows :

1. The appearance to Mary Magdalene (John, Appendix to Mark). According to the Marcan Appendix this appearance was the " first."

2. The appearance to the women on their way to the disciples (Matt.). The relation to (1) is considered below.

3. The appearance to St. Peter (Luke, Paul). St. Paul doubtless had the fact from St. Peter himself. St. Luke probably had it from St. Paul. But it was known from the beginning.[3]

4. The appearance to the two disciples on the road to Emmaus (Luke, Appendix to Mark). St. Luke gives the detailed account.

---

[1] This should be partially qualified in the case of St. John, who does exhibit an evidential purpose (chap. xx. 31 ; xxi. 24).

[2] Each Evangelist would have been ready to endorse the concluding words in St. John: " There are also many other things which Jesus did," etc. (xxi. 5 ; cf. xx. 31).

[3] Luke xxiv. 34. St. Mark may have had this appearance in view in the words : " Go, tell His disciples and Peter " (xvi. 7).

5. The appearance to the assembled disciples
in the evening (Luke, John, Paul, Appendix to
Mark). The details are given in St. Luke and St.
John.

These five appearances all occurred on the day of
Resurrection.

6. The second appearance to the eleven, " eight
days after " (John). St. John had told how, on the
previous occasion, Thomas was not present. The
doubt of Thomas was now removed.

7. An appearance to seven disciples at the Lake
of Galilee (John).

8. The great appearance to over five hundred
brethren at once (Paul). This, as above said, is
probably identical with the " appointed " meeting
in Galilee, when the " eleven " received their Lord's .
great Commission (Matt).

9. An appearance to St. James (Paul).

10. The final appearance to the eleven (Paul),
identical with the meeting of Jesus with His disciples
prior to His Ascension (Luke in Gospel and Acts ;
Appendix to Mark).

It will be perceived from this enumeration that
there were in all no fewer than *five* appearances of
Jesus—half of the total number—to the Apostles,
when all, or a majority, were present ; in one instance at a large gathering of over five hundred.
Of the remaining instances, three were private
(to Mary, St. Peter, St James) : one was to two

disciples on a journey; one was to the group of women. St. Matthew probably introduces the last because of the message then repeated to meet the Lord in Galilee. St. Luke, as shown, confines himself to the meetings in and about Jerusalem. St. Paul dwells naturally for his purpose on the appearances to the Apostles, including that to James, and the meeting with the five hundred. St. John fills up from his reminiscences what the others had left untold—the tender scene with the Magdalene, the second appearance to the Apostles, the appearance to the seven in Galilee. It all seems very natural. The pieces of the puzzle are perhaps not so hard to put together after all.

The circumstances of the several appearances must now be more carefully investigated, with a view to the further elucidation of their *nature* and *reality*. But, first, there are certain threads of the Synoptical narratives which require to be gathered up, and related to what follows.

1. Two of the Evangelists, St. Matthew and St. Mark, agree that the women at the tomb *received a message* to give to the disciples.[1] St. Luke does not mention this message, yet relates: " They returned from the tomb, and told all these things to the eleven, and to all the rest " [2] (the implication of a wider company should be noted). In the report of the words spoken by the angels to the

---

[1] Matt. xxviii. 7 ; Mark xvi. 7.   [2] Luke xxiv. 9.

women, however, there is an important variation in St. Luke, which needs consideration. In the two other Synoptics, the women are directed to tell the disciples that Jesus goes before them into Galilee, and that there they will see Him. Instead of this message, St. Luke reads : " Remember how He spake unto you when He was yet in Galilee, saying that the Son of Man must be delivered up unto the hands of sinful men and be crucified, and the third day rise again. And they remembered His words." [1] In St. Matthew, further, the words which in St. Mark appear in connexion with the direction about Galilee (" as He said unto you ") [2] are transferred to the announcement of the Resurrection (" as He said "), [3] and the angel's message closes with the statement, " Lo, I have told you." The difficulty of deriving either of these forms from the other is obvious (the word " Galilee " occurring in both should not mislead). The simple explanation seems to be that it is not the design of St. Luke to relate the appearances in Galilee (cf., however, Acts i. 3 ; " appearing to them by the space of forty days ") ; he therefore omits the part of the message bearing on this point. For the rest, Jesus did do both things there stated : (1) announce when in Galilee His approaching death and Resurrection [4] (so in Matt.), and St. Luke

---

[1] Luke xxiv. 6–8.   [2] Mark xvi. 7.   [3] Matt. xxviii. 6.
[4] Cf. Matt. xvi. 21 ; xvii. 9–13, etc.

simply repeats His words; and (2) announce that He would meet His disciples in Galilee [1] (" as He said unto you," Mark). This second part St. Luke passes over.

2. In the close of his narrative of the Resurrection, St. Matthew gives *the sequel to his story of the guard* at the tomb [2] previously alluded to. Certain of the guard, hastening to the city, told the chief priests what had happened. These, after counsel with the elders, bribed the soldiers to spread the report that the disciples had stolen the body of Jesus while they (the guard) slept, promising to use their interest with Pilate to secure them from harm. This episode, as was before seen, is rejected by the critics as fabulous. Yet it is difficult to believe that a narrative so circumstantial could be simple invention,[3] or have no foundation in fact. Nor are the grounds alleged adequate to sustain this view of it. The central point in the story— the charge of stealing the body—is evidently historical. It is given as a current report when the Gospel was written,[4] and is independently attested.[5]

---

[1] Matt. xxvi. 32; Mark xiv. 28.

[2] Matt. xxvii. 11-15. Cf. chap. xxvii. 62-66.

[3] Professor Lake thinks that the episode has " neither intrinsic nor traditional probability." It is, in his view, " nothing more than a fragment of controversy " between Jews and Gentiles, " in which each imputed unworthy motives to the other, and stated suggestions as established fact " (p. 180).   [4] Matt. xxviii. 15.

[5] Justin Martyr, *Dialogue with Trypho*, 108; Tertullian, *On Spectacles*, 30.

As giving the Jewish version of the Resurrection, it has value as a left-hand testimony to the fact of the grave being found empty. When it is asked, Is it likely that the soldiers should accept a bribe to plead guilty to a military offence—sleeping on duty—which was punishable by death ?[1] it is overlooked that the breach of discipline had already been committed in their flight from the tomb, and admission that the tomb was open and the body gone. The theft by the disciples was only a pretext to cover an event which both soldiers and priests were aware had really a more marvellous character. The case would be presented in a truer light to Pilate, and the soldiers screened. It was probably from some of the guards themselves—led, like the centurion, to say, " Truly this man was the Son of God," [2]—that the facts were ascertained.[3]

This leads to the consideration of the distinct appearances.

1. Little use has up to this point been made of the testimony of St. John. It is now necessary to consider that testimony in its relation to the Synoptics, as embodying the narrative of the first of our Lord's recorded appearances—that to *Mary Mag-*

---

[1] Lake, p. 178.   [2] Mark xv. 39.

[3] Dr. Forrest, in his *Christ of History and Experience*, says : This " incident related by Matthew . . . though it is not corroborated in any of the other Gospels, has, I think, every mark of probability " (p. 145). Cf. Alford on Matt. xxvii. 62–66.

dalene.[1]   St. John has the supreme qualification as a witness that he himself was *magna pars* in the transactions he records.   His narrative has an autoptic character.   Part of its design apparently is to give greater precision to certain events which the other Gospels had more or less generalized.   It is a piece of testimony of the first importance.

In the story of the appearance to Mary Magdalene, St. John so far goes with the Synoptics that he tells how Mary Magdalene came in the early morning to the tomb of Jesus, and found the stone taken away.[2]   Mention is not made of companions, but probably at least one other is implied in Mary's words : " They have taken away the Lord out of the tomb, and *we* know not where they have laid Him." [3]   The same words may suggest that, either by her own inspection or that of others, Mary had ascertained that the tomb was empty—not simply open.

But here St. John diverges.   We learn from him how, concluding that the body had been removed, Mary at once ran to carry the news to St. Peter and St. John.   It was still very early, and the disciples had to be sought for in their private—perhaps separate—lodgings (ver. 10).   Aroused by her tale, they lost not a moment in hastening to the

---

[1] John xx. 11–18.
[2] Ver. 1.   [3] Ver. 2.

spot.[1] St. John—for he only can be meant by
" the other disciple "[2]—outran St. Peter, and coming first to the tomb, stooped and looked in, and
saw (βλέπει) the linen cloths (ὀθόνια) lying, but
did not go farther. St. Peter followed, but, with
characteristic energy, at once entered, and beheld
(θεωρεῖ, implying careful note), not simply the
disposition of the cloths, but the peculiarity of the
napkin for the head lying rolled up in a place by
itself.[3] St. John then found courage to enter, and
" having seen, believed."[4] It is a weakening of
this expression to suppose it to mean simply, " believed that the tomb was empty." Both disciples
believed this. But with a flash of true discernment
St. John grasped the significance of what he saw,
viz., that Jesus had risen—a truth to which the
Scriptures had not yet led him.[5] St. Peter, it is
implied, though wondering,[6] had still not attained
to this confidence. The two disciples then returned
home.[7]

Meanwhile Mary Magdalene had come back, and
was " standing without at the tomb weeping."[8]
Afterwards she too stooped and looked into the

[1] Ver. 3–10. [2] Vers. 2, 3, 8.
[3] Ver. 7. Mr. Latham's ingenious reasoning from the
disposition of the grave-cloths to the manner of the Resurrection should be studied in his *Risen Master*, chaps. i–iii.
[4] Ver. 8. [5] Ver. 9.
[6] Cf. Luke xxii. 12, below.
[7] Ver. 10. [8] Ver. 11.

tomb, and had, like the other women, a " vision of angels "—in her case " two angels in white raiment," one at the head, the other at the foot, of the ledge or slab where the body of Jesus had lain.[1] Then came the meeting with the Lord described in the succeeding verses. At first Mary took the person who addressed her for the gardener, and besought him, if it was he who had borne away her Lord from the tomb, to tell her where he had laid Him.[2] Little trace here of the *hallucinée*, whose passion, according to Renan, " gave to the world a resuscitated god."[3] Christ's tender word " Mary " illuminated her at once as to who He was, and with the exclamation " Rabboni," she would have clasped Him, had He permitted her.

The words with which the Risen Lord in this interview gently checked the movement of Mary at once to worship and to detain Him—to hold Him, now restored to her, as if never more to let Him go—have been the subject of sufficiently diverse interpretations. " Touch me not " ($\mu\acute{\eta}$ $\mu o\upsilon$ $\ddot{\alpha}\pi\tau o\upsilon$; R.V. marg., " Take not hold on Me "), Jesus said, " for I am not yet ascended unto My Father ; but go unto My brethren, and say to them, I ascend unto My Father and your Father, and My God and your God."[4] The meaning that lies on the surface is : " Do not hold me now, for I am not yet ascended

---

[1] Vers. 11-13, see the plates of the tomb in Latham.
[2] Ver. 15. [3] *l'ie de Jésus*, p. 434. [4] Ver. 17.

unto My Father, but go at once unto My brethren,"
etc. But the terms of the message to the brethren
("Say unto them, I ascend," etc.) show that a
deeper reason lay behind. "Tell them," its purport is, "that I am risen; the same, yet entered on
a higher (the Ascension) life, in which old relations
cannot be renewed, but better ones begin."[1]

If this striking narrative of St. John stood alone,
it would be sufficiently attested, but it is corroborated by two notices which probably are independent of it. The Appendix to St. Mark tells of the
early morning appearance to Mary Magdalene;[2]
St. Luke records the visit of St. Peter to the tomb,
in language closely resembling St. John's, with an
indication later that he was not alone. St. Luke
xxiv. 12, reads: "But Peter arose and ran into
the tomb; and stooping and looking in, he seeth
(βλέπει) the linen cloths (ὀθόνια) by themselves,
and he departed to his home, wondering at
that which was come to pass." In verse 24, the
disciples journeying to Emmaus say: "And certain of them that were with us went to the tomb,
and found it even as the women had said: but

---

[1] The chief interpretations of the passage can be seen
in Godet, Com. on St. John, iii. pp. 311–13, and in Latham,
ut supra, pp. 419–20. Godet takes it to mean: "I have
not reached the state in which I shall be able to live with
you in the communion I promised you" (p. 311).

[2] On the supposed dependence on St. John, cf. remark
above.

Him they saw not." [1]   On the ground of its absence
from certain Western texts, the former passage (ver.
12) is regarded by textual critics with suspicion.[2]
This doubt does not attach to verse 24, which plainly
has in view the visit described by St. John. Its
genuineness, in turn, supports that of verse 12,
where St. Peter only is mentioned. It may reasonably be supposed that St. John, in his fuller narrative,
has the aim of rectifying a certain inexactitude in
St. Luke's summary account. St. Luke, e.g.,
speaks of St. Peter, at the tomb, as " stooping and
looking in "   St. John, the disciple who accompanied
St. Peter, explains that, while this was true of himself (cf. chap. xx. 5), St. Peter did more, actually
entering the tomb and inspecting the contents.
In his consecutive account, he makes clear also the
precise time of this visit.

2. At this point a question of some nicety arises
as to the relation of this appearance to Mary Magdalene, and *the appearance to the women recorded*
in St. Matthew xxviii. 9, 10, which stands next upon
our list. Are these appearances different ? Or

---

[1] Meyer remarks : " Of the ' other disciple ' of John
xx. 3, Luke says nothing, but, according to ver. 24, does
not exclude him " (*Com. in loc.*).

[2] The preponderance of early MSS. authority sustains
the passage. Godet, who, in his *Com. on St. Luke* (ii. p. 352)
upholds the genuineness, treats it in his *Com. on St. John*
(iii. p. 308) as " a gloss borrowed from St. John." Had
it been so, it would surely have avoided the appearance
of contradiction !

is the second (that in Matthew) merely a generalized form of the first (that in John)? The latter is the view taken by many scholars.[1] In favour of it is the fact that only two women, Mary Magdalene and the other Mary, are mentioned in St. Matthew's narrative.[2] We know, however, that there were other women present, and there is a marked contrast in the circumstances in the two narratives. The women in St. Matthew are already on their way to tell the disciples; they hold Jesus by the feet, and are apparently unrebuked (the act was *only* one of worship); the message, too, is different. The appearance to Mary may well be grouped (probably is) with that of the other women; it is not so easy to identify the, latter with Mary's solitary experience. If, on the other hand, the appearances are taken to be distinct, a difficulty arises as to the order of time. The appearance to the women coming from the tomb would now seem to claim precedence over that to Mary, who had in the interval gone to Jerusalem and had returned. There is nothing absolutely to preclude this, if the note of order in the Appendix to St. Mark (" appeared first to Mary Magdalene ") be surrendered. Some, accordingly, do place the appearance to the other women first.[3]

---

[1] E.g., Ebrard, Godet, Alford, Swete.   [2] Ver. 1.
[3] E.g., Milligan, *The Resur. of our Lord*, pp. 259-60.

But even on the ordinarily received view that the appearance to Mary Magdalene was the prior, the problem, when the circumstances are fairly considered, does not seem insoluble. Both appearances took place in early morning, with at most an hour or two between them. The disciples, mostly lodging apart—in Jerusalem,[1] in Bethany, elsewhere [2]—could not be convened till later. The women, after their first hurried flight (cf. Mark xvi. 8) must have paused to regain their self-possession, to confer with one another on what they had seen and heard, to consider how they should proceed in conveying their tidings to the still scattered disciples. In such a pause, their hearts aflame with love and holy desire, Jesus, who a little earlier had made Himself known to Mary in the garden, appeared to them. Even before He approached a single Apostle, He disclosed Himself to this company of faithful hearts. His " All hail ! " and the renewed commission to the disciples sealed the message at the tomb.

It is not unlikely that, before long, on her way back to the city, Mary Magdalene joined her sisters, and that, after interchange of experiences, the errand to the disciples was undertaken by the women together. Keen indeed must have been the chill to their enthusiasm at the reception their message

---

[1] As St. Peter and St. John above.
[2] Two were from Emmaus.

met with when they did deliver it. Their words received no credence : were treated as " idle talk." [1] That the tomb was found empty, the Apostles did not dispute ; but stories of visions of angels and appearances of Jesus they refused to accept. There was astonishment, but not belief. Yet it is this sceptical circle, antipathetic to visionary experiences, in which belief in the Resurrection is supposed spontaneously to have arisen through visions of their own.

3. It must have been still early on this eventful day, probably soon after the Apostle's visit to the tomb, and while he was still brooding on what had happened, that the third appearance of Jesus took place—*the appearance to St. Peter*, attested by both, St. Paul [2] and St. Luke. [3] The critics, as will be found, transfer this appearance from Jerusalem to Galilee, but without a shadow of a valid reason. It was in harmony with the tender, considerate spirit displayed by Jesus in all these manifestations that such an appearance should be granted, so soon after the Resurrection, to the disciple who had denied, yet who so devotedly loved Him—whom He Himself had named the " Rock." [4] Like the appearance to St. James at a later period, the meeting was entirely private. It can only be

[1] Luke xxiv. 10, 11, 22, 23. Cf. Mark xvi. 9-11.
[2] 1 Cor. xv. 5.   [3] Luke xxiv. 34.
[4] Matt. xvi. 18 ; John i. 42.

conjectured how, with another look, reproachful perhaps, but gracious and forgiving, the memory was banished of that look turned upon St. Peter in the High Priest's palace, which had overwhelmed him with such sorrow.[1] The great stone was now rolled away from his heart, as before the stone had been rolled from the tomb. The transformation which this appearance of Christ wrought in the Apostle is reflected in the excitement which the report of it created in the circle of the disciples. " The Lord hath risen indeed and hath appeared to Simon."[2] The disciples might disbelieve the women ; they could not doubt the reality of the experience of St. Peter. The " conversion " which Jesus had predicted was realized, and thereafter the Apostle was to " strengthen " his brethren.[3]

4. As it is with the appearance to St. Peter, so it is with the other appearance which may be associated with this, as of the same private order—the *appearance to St. James.*

It is among the latest of the appearances, as that to Peter is among the earliest. With regard to both,

---

[1] Luke xxii. 61.

[2] Luke xxiv. 34. Prof. Lake thinks it " uncertain " whether Simon Peter or another is intended in this passage —a characteristic excess of scepticism. He cannot believe that St. Luke has in view the appearance to Cephas referred to by St. Paul. He prefers, " with the courage of despair," as he calls it, to " think that St. Luke himself did not write " the passage (pp. 101–3).

[3] Luke xxii. 32.   [4] 1 Cor. xv. 7.

while the facts are well-attested, no particulars are given. It is not doubted that the person intended in St. Paul's notice is the well-known James, the " brother of the Lord." [1] This of itself explains much. James, so far as is known, was not a believer in Jesus up to the time of the Crucifixion.[2] Yet immediately after the Ascension, he, and the other brethren of Jesus, are found in the company of the disciples.[3] Thereafter he became a " pillar "[4]—finally the chief personage—in the Church at Jerusalem.[5] He ranked with the Apostles.[6] What could explain such a change, save that, like the other Apostles, he had " seen the Lord ? "[7] Christ's appearance to St. James was not simply His revelation to His own family—His kinsfolk according to the flesh—but was the qualification for lifelong Apostolic service. St. James exercised an authority at Jerusalem hardly second to that of St. Paul among the Churches of the Gentiles.

The remaining appearances will introduce us to the problems connected with the nature of the Resurrection body of the Lord.[8]

---

[1] Gal. i. 19. Cf. Matt. xiii. 35 ; Mark vi. 3.
[2] Cf. John vii. 5.   [3] Acts i. 14.   [4] Gal. iii. 9.
[5] Acts xii. 17 ; xv. 13 ; xxi. 18.
[6] Gal. i. 19 ; ii. 9 ; 1 Cor. ix. 5.   [7] Cf. 1 Cor. ix. 1.
[8] Cf. Hegisippus in Eusebius, *Ecc. Hist.*, ii. 23.   There is a legend about St. James in the *Gospel according to the Hebrews* (cf. Westcott, *Introd. to Gospels*, p. 463 ; Lightfoot, *Galatians*, p. 274), to which, however, little, if any, weight can be attached.   Apocryphal ideas will be considered later.

THE SIGNIFICANCE OF THE APPEAR ANCES—THE RISEN BODY

VII

THE SIGNIFICANCE OF THE APPEARANCES
THE RISEN BODY

THE appearances of Jesus already considered—those, viz., to Mary Magdalene, to the women, to St. Peter, on the day of Resurrection, and that to St. James later—were all of a private or semi-private nature. Isolated, under varying conditions, designed for personal comfort and confirmation, taking place well-nigh simultaneously, the manifestations to one and another on the Resurrection day afforded no room for self-deception, or for collusion, or the contagious action of sympathy. It would seem as if, on this first day, by manifestations to individuals chosen for their peculiar receptiveness or representative character, Jesus desired to lay a broad basis for certainty in His Rising, before He appeared to His disciples as a body.

Another example of this semi-private form of manifestation to which attention must now be directed was the appearance of Jesus to *the two disciples on their way to Emmaus,* the full account

of which is furnished by St. Luke.[1] The name
of only one of these favoured disciples is given—
Cleopas :[2] otherwise both are unknown. Chosen
for this honour as representatives of the wider circle
of disciples, doubtless also for the susceptibility
discerned in them for the reception of Christ's
communications, they form a link with the general
Apostolic company. From it they had just come,
after hearing the reports of certain of the women
and of others who had visited the tomb,[3] and to
it they returned after their own meeting with
Jesus, to find the company in excitement at the
news of the Lord's appearance to St. Peter, and to
witness another appearance of the Master.[4] Theirs
was the singular privilege, shared, so far as is
known, by St. Peter only, of beholding the Risen
Lord twice on one day !

The story of St. Luke is simple and direct, with
every internal mark of truthfulness. The disciples were on their way to Emmaus, a village
about two hours' walk from Jerusalem,[5] when
Jesus overtook them, and questioned them as to
the nature of their communings. Their inability
to recognize Him is explained by the statement :
" Their eyes were holden that they should not
know Him."[6] Their simple recital of the events of

---

[1] Luke xxiv. 12–35.   [2] Ver. 18.   [3] Vers. 22–24.
[4] Vers. 34–36.
[5] Ver. 13 ; cf. Josephus, *Jewish War*, vii. 6, 6.   [6] Ver. 16.

the past few days and expression of their disappointed hopes—" We hoped that it was He who should redeem Israel "[1]—with their mention of the women's tale of the " vision of angels, who said that He was alive," [2] gave Jesus the opportunity of reproving their unbelief, and of expounding to them in His own way the meaning of the Scriptures regarding Himself.[3]   As the day was closing, they constrained Jesus to abide with them ; then, at the evening meal, as Jesus blessed and brake the bread, and gave it to them, " their eyes were opened and they knew Him ; and He vanished out of their sight." [4]   Recalling how their hearts had burned within them as He opened to them the Scriptures, they hastily rose, and returned at once to Jerusalem.[5] According to the Appendix to St. Mark, their testimony, like that of the women earlier, was not at first believed [6]—a fact very credible when the strangeness of their story, and the difficulty of harmonizing the appearance at Emmaus with

---

[1] Ver. 21.   [2] Ver. 23.

[3] Vers. 25-27.   The Lord's exposition of the Scriptures here and later (vers. 44-46) may have turned on the sufferings and fate of righteous men and prophets in all ages, and on the predictions of the future triumph and glory of the Sufferer in Ps. xxii. (vers. 22-31), and Is. liii.   Psalms like the 16th and prophecies like Zech. xiii. would also have place (cf. Hengstenberg, *Christologie*, iv. App. iv.).

[4] Vers. 30-31.   [5] Vers. 32-33.

[6] Mark xvi. 12, 13.

that to St. Peter at Jerusalem, are considered.[1]

It is apparent from many parts of his Gospel that St. Luke had access to a Jerusalem tradition of primitive origin and high value, and this narrative, which probably took shape at the time from the report of the disciples,[2] is, in its clear, straightforward character, evidently one of the best preserved parts of that tradition. Critics, accordingly, while of course rejecting its testimony to the bodily appearance of Jesus, commonly treat the Emmaus narrative with considerable respect. As examples, Renan, after his manner, takes the picturesque story simply as it stands, transforming the stranger into "a pious man well versed in the Scriptures," whose gesture in the breaking of bread at the evening repast vividly recalled Jesus, and plunged the disciples into tender thoughts. When they awoke from their reverie, the stranger was gone.[3] A. Meyer sees in the appearance to Simon and the naming of Cleopas and Emmaus evidence that St. Luke's source contained "valuable old material." His

---

[1] It is told in Luke xxiv. 41 that, even when the Lord Himself appeared among them, the Apostles and disciples "disbelieved for joy."

[2] Cf. Latham, *The Risen Master*, pp. 135-7.

[3] *Les Apôtres*, pp. 18-21. Renan's descrption is characteristic. "How often had they not seen their beloved Master, in that hour, forget the burden of the day, and, in the abandon of gay conversation, and enlivened by several sips of excellent wine, speak to them of the fruit of the vine," etc. (p. 11).

chief objection is that St. Paul does not mention an incident which, if true, must have been " of priceless significance as a proof of the Resurrection." [1] Professor Lake allows that the story " reads as though it were based on fact," and thinks it " is probably a genuine remnant of the original tradition of the Church at Jerusalem, which has suffered a little in the process of transmission." [2] It is supposed to preserve a recollection of appearances in the neighbourhood of Jerusalem, afterwards woven into connexion with the Apostles (thus also A. Meyer). The reference to the appearance to Simon, assumed to be Galilean, is excised. [3] Against these arbitrary conjectures, the simplicity and directness of the narrative—its " air of reality "—sufficiently speak. [4]

The real points of difficulty in the narrative are those which touch on the mystery of the Lord's Resurrection body. Such are (1) His non-recognition by the disciples through " their eyes " being " holden " (or, as in the Appendix to St. Mark, His appearance to them " in another form " [5]) ; (2) His vanishing from their sight at the table ; (3) His appearing on the same evening at Jerusalem. These points are

[1] *Die Auferstehung Christi*, pp. 132–3.
[2] *Res. of Jesus Christ*, pp. 218–19.
[3] Ibid. pp. 103, 219.
[4] On general objections to the narrative cf. Loof's *Die Auferstehungsberichte und ihr Wert*, pp. 27–8.
[5] Mark xvi. 12.

better held over till all the facts of a similar nature are in view.

The time had now arrived when these private appearances of Jesus were to give place to His more public manifestations of Himself to His disciples. Accordingly, still on the Resurrection-evening, and in connexion with the visit of the Emmaus disciples just described, we come to the *first* in order of the important series of *the appearances of the Lord to His assembled Apostles.* This, as in a marked degree typical, will repay careful study.

1. The witnesses to this *first appearance to the Apostles* are St. Luke [1] and St. John,[2] supported by St. Paul.[3] The story, in St. Luke, is the continuation of the Emmaus narrative; in St. John it is a distinct episode, and furnishes in its commencement the important detail that, when Jesus appeared, " the doors were shut where the disciples were, for fear of the Jews." [4] This makes more emphatic the marvel of Christ's sudden appearance in the midst of the disciples, which yet is implied in both narratives. " Jesus," St. Luke says, " Himself stood ($\check{\epsilon}\sigma\tau\eta$) in the midst of them."[5] St. John speaks similarly: " Jesus came and stood in the midst."[6] This practical identity of lan-

---

[1] Luke xxiv. 36–43.
[2] John xx. 19–23.
[3] 1 Cor. xv. 5.
[4] John xx. 19.
[5] Luke xxiv. 36.
[6] John xx. 19.

guage in an undoubted part of the text should predispose us to consider favourably the two succeeding clauses in St. Luke, likewise identical with, or closely akin to St. John's, on which doubt is cast by their absence from some Western texts. They are these : (1) Ver. 36 reads, as in St. John [1] · " And saith unto them, Peace be unto you." (2) Ver. 40 reads : " And when He had said this, He showed them His hands and His feet," where St. John has : " And when He had said this He showed unto them His hands and His side." [2] The passages are here accepted as genuine ; [3] but whether expressed or not, the showing of the hands and the feet in the latter is implied in St. Luke's preceding words : " See My hands and My feet," etc.[4]

Up to a certain point, therefore, the two narratives agree almost verbally. That of St. John an immediate witness, confirms that of St. Luke and with it supports the authenticity of St. Luke's narrative generally. The astonishment and doubt which the Lord's sudden appearance occasioned

[1] John xx. 19.   [2] John xx. 20.

[3] Alford's notes may be quoted. On ver. 36 : " Possibly from John ; but as the whole is nearly related to that narrative, and the authority for the omission weak, Tischendorf is certainly not justified in expunging it." On ver. 40 : " Had this been interpolated from St. John, we certainly should have found ' feet ' altered by some to ' side,' either here only, or in ver. 39 also." The R.V. retains both clauses in the text.

[4] Luke xxiv. 39.

is reflected in both. St. Luke's language is the more vivid. " They were terrified and affrighted, and supposed that they beheld a spirit." [1] Even after the Lord's reassurances, and His invitation, " Handle Me, and see : for a spirit hath not flesh and bones, as ye behold Me having," it is declared, " They still disbelieved for joy, and wondered." [2] The removal of doubt is implied in St. John in Christ's showing of His hands and His side, and the " joy " is corroborated in the words : " The disciples therefore were glad when they saw the Lord." [3] The whole account is psychologically most natural, and sheds vivid light by contrast on the theories which see the origin of belief in the Resurrection in an eager credulity and proneness to mistake hallucinations for reality on the part of the Apostles.

At this point St. Luke and St. John part company, each giving an incident not related by the other. St. Luke tells how, at His own request, the disciples gave Jesus a piece of a broiled fish [the words " and of a honey-comb " are doubtful] and He " ate before them " [4] (a like " eating " seems implied in the later scene in St. John at the Lake of Galilee).[5] St. John, on the other hand, tells of a renewed commission to the Apostles, and of how Jesus " breathed on them, and said unto them,

[1] Ver. 37. [2] Ver. 41. [3] John xx. 20.
[4] Luke xxiv. 43. [5] John xxi. 4-13.

Receive ye [the] Holy Spirit. Whosesoever sins ye forgive, they are forgiven unto them ; whosesoever sins ye retain, they are retained." [1] Into the controversies connected with these solemn words, this is not the place to enter. It may be that here, as elsewhere, Jesus is contemplating the existence of a spiritual Society, and is investing His Apostles with disciplinary authority to deal with sins which affect the standing of members in that Society.[2] Or the deeper thought may be that the remission or retention of sins is bound up *ipso facto* with the reception or rejection of the message which He commits to the Apostles to bear. Whatever the nature of the authority, the text makes plain that its exercise is conditioned by the possession of the Holy Spirit. It is not necessary to assume that the actual imparting of the Spirit was delayed till Pentecost. The act of breathing and the words used by Jesus imply that the Spirit was *then* given in a measure, if not in the fulness of the later affusion.[3] St. John, too, knew that the Spirit was not given till Christ was glorified.[4]

In this incident, as in the earlier appearances, while proof is given of the reality of Christ's risen

---

[1] John xx. 21-3.

[2] Cf. Matt. xviii. 17, 18. See also Latham, *ut supra*, pp. 168–74.

[3] " Arrha Pentecostes " (Bengel). " That preparatory communication, that anticipatory Pentecost " (Godet).

[4] John vii. 39.

body, and of its identity with the body that was crucified and buried, not less plain evidence is afforded of the changed conditions under which that body now existed. The fact is meanwhile, again, only noted. When, however, the critics import into these narratives a contradiction with St. Paul's conception of Christ's Resurrection body,[1] and, to heighten the variance, arbitrarily transfer the appearance to "the twelve" mentioned by St. Paul in 1 Cor. xv. 5, to Galilee, it must be pointed out that they not only break with a sound Jerusalem tradition, of which the Apostle must have been perfectly aware, but assert what, on the face of it, is an incredibility. What motive or occasion can be suggested for a convening of "the twelve" (or eleven) in Galilee to receive an appearance?[2] And how difficult to conceive of the simultaneous experience of such a vision by a band of men so brought together! Better with A. Meyer, to cast doubt on the appearance altogether.[3]

[1] Thus Henson (*Hibbert Journal*, 1903-4, pp. 476-93, Weizsäcker, A. Meyer, Loisy (*Les Evangiles*, ii. p. 772), etc. On the other hand, cf. Loofs, *ut supra*, pp. 27-9, 33.

[2] According to Loisy, it was St. Peter, who had one day seen Jesus when fishing on the Lake of Tiberias (see below), who "no doubt [!] gathered the eleven, and kindled with his ardour their wavering faith" (ii. p. 224).

[3] *Ut supra*, p. 139. After disposing of all details, Meyer concludes that there is a "kernel" of truth in the story The vision theory is discussed in next chapter.

2. Eight days after this first appearance—St. John here again being witness—*a second appearance of Jesus to the Apostles* took place in the same chamber, and under the like conditions ("the doors being shut").[1] The peculiar feature of this second meeting was the removal of the doubt of St. Thomas, who, it is related, had not been present on the earlier occasion.[2] St. Thomas, in a spirit which the "modern" mind should appreciate, refused to believe in so extraordinary a fact as the Resurrection of the Lord in the body on the mere report of others, and demanded indubitable sensible evidence of the miracle for himself. "Except I shall see in His hands the print of the nails, and put my finger into the print of the nails, and put my hand into His side, I will not believe."[3] Graciously, at this second appearance, Jesus gave the doubting Apostle the evidence he asked—"Reach hither thy hand,"[4] etc.—though, as the event proved, the sign was not needed. The faith of the disciple was greater than he thought, and the sight and words of Jesus sufficed, without actual examination, to bring him to his Lord's feet in adoring acknowledgment. The love and reverence that lay beneath his doubts came in a surge of instantaneous devotion to the surface: "My Lord and my God."[5] Yet, as Jesus reminded him, there is a higher faith still

[1] John xix. 24–9   [2] John xx. 24.   [3] Ver. 25.
[4] Ver. 27.   [5] Ver. 28.

—that which does not need even seeing, but apprehends intuitively that in the nature of the case nothing else could be true of One in whom the Eternal Life was revealed. " Because thou hast seen Me, thou hast believed ; blessed are they that have not seen, and yet have believed." [1]

The confidence instinctively awakened by this striking narrative of the Lord's treatment of a doubting spirit is not disturbed by the inability that may be felt to explain why the Apostles should still be at Jerusalem a whole week after they had received the direction to meet the Lord in Galilee. Various reasons might be suggested for the delay. It appears from St. Matthew that place and time of the Galilean meeting were definitely " appointed." [2] There was therefore no need for departure till the time drew near. It was, besides, the week of the Passover feast, and there was urgent cause why the Apostles, in the new circumstances that had arisen, should remain at Jerusalem to bear their own testimony, allay doubts, meet inquirers, check false rumours and calumnies. [3] When they did journey northwards it would probably still be in company. The departure may well have taken place in the course of the week succeeding that renewed appearance of Jesus on the eighth day. Very significant must

[1] Ver. 29.　　　　　[2] Matt. xxviii. 18.
[3] Godet suggests as a reason " the obstinacy of Thomas " (*St. John*, iii. pp. 319, 330).

that second meeting on " the first day of the week "—
the anniversary of the Rising—have been felt by
the disciples to be ! It consecrated it for them
anew as " the Lord's Day " ! [1]

3. In harmony with this view of the succession
of events, the scene of manifestation is now transferred to Galilee, and *the third appearance* of the Lord
to His disciples takes place, as recorded in St. John
xxi, on the shore of the Lake of Galilee (" Sea of
Tiberias ").[2] The chapter (xxi.) is a supplement
to the rest of the Gospel, but is so evidently
Johannine in character that, with the exception
of the endorsement in verses 24-5, it may safely
be accepted as from the pen of the beloved disciple.[3]
Seven disciples were present on this occasion, of
whom five are named (" Simon Peter, Thomas,
Nathanael, the Sons of Zebedee "). [4] All five are
Apostles, if, as is probable, Nathanael is to be
identified with Bartholomew. This creates the like-
lihood that " the two other of His disciples " were
Apostles also—unnamed, perhaps, as Luthardt
suggests,[5] because not elsewhere mentioned in the

---

[1] Rev. i. 10.   [2] John xxi. 1.

[3] " Some (e.g. Zahn) prefer to take the chapter as the
work of a disciple, or disciples, of St. John. But style,
allusions, marks of eye-witness speak to its being from
the same hand as the rest of the Gospel (thus Lightfoot,
Meyer, Godet, Alford, etc.). The attestation (ver. 24),
covers this chapter equally with the others. The Gospel
never circulated without it.

[4] Ver. 2.   [5] *Com. on St. John*, iii. p. 358.

Gospel. At every point the life-like touches in the story attest the writer as an eye-witness. The disciples had spent a night of fruitless toil in fishing. At break of day, Jesus appeared to them on the shore, and, as yet unrecognized, bade them cast their net on the right side of the boat.[1] The unprecedented draught of fishes which rewarded their effort revealed at once to St. John the presence of the Lord. "It is the Lord," he said.[2] St. Peter, on hearing the words, girt his fisher's coat about him ("for he was naked"), and cast himself into the sea, while the others dragged the net to shore. [3] Arrived there, they found a fire of coals, with fish laid on it, and bread ; after other fish had been brought, Jesus invited them to eat, and with His own hand distributed the bread and the fish.[4] It is remarked that, whilst the disciples now knew it was the Lord, none durst inquire of Him, "Who art Thou?"[5] It seems implied, though it is not directly stated, that Jesus Himself shared in the meal. The scene that followed of St. Peter's reinstatement (the three-fold question, answering to the three-fold denial, with its subtle play on the word "lovest,"[6] St. Peter's replies, Christ's "Feed My lambs," "Feed My sheep") is familiar to every reader of Scripture.[7]

It need hardly be said, that, with all its delicate

[1] Ver. 4.   [2] Ver. 7.   [3] Vers. 7, 8.
[4] Vers. 9–13.   [5] Ver. 12.
[6] ἀγαπᾷς (vers. 15, 16) ; φιλεῖς (ver. 17). St. Peter uses φιλῶ.   [7] Vers. 15–19.

marks of truth, this narrative of the Fourth Gospel meets with short shrift at the hands of the critics. Its symbolical character is thought to rob it of all claim to historicity. The theories propounded regarding it are as various as the minds that conceive them. One curious speculation, adopted by Harnack,[1] is that St. John xxi. represents the lost ending of St. Mark. Professor Lake thinks that " there is certainly not a little to be said for this hypothesis."[2] In reality it has *nothing* in its favour, beyond the probability that the lost section of St. Mark contained the account of some appearance in Galilee.[3] Most take the first part of the chapter to be a version, with adaptations, of St. Luke's story of the miraculous draught of fishes. Strauss sees in it a combination of this " legend " in St. Luke with that of St. Peter walking on the sea.[4] Only in this case St. Peter does *not* walk on the sea. The newest tendency is to find in it a reminiscence of the appearance of Jesus to St. Peter, transferred to the Lake of Galilee.[5] The second

---

[1] *Chronologie*, i. pp. 696 ff. Harnack follows Rohrbach. Others see the lost conclusion of St. Mark behind Matt. xxviii. 16–20.

[2] *Ut supra*, p. 143.

[3] As already said, style, names (Nathanael, Cana in Galilee, Didymus, etc.), and whole cast of the narrative speak for Johannine authorship and rebut this Marcan theory. [4] *New Life of Jesus*, ii. pp. 131–2.

[5] Thus, e.g. Loisy: " He [St. Peter] had seen Jesus one day in the dawn when fishing on the Lake of Tiberias," etc. (*ut supra*, p. 224).

part of the story Renan accounts for by " dreams."
(" One day Peter, dreaming, believed that he heard
Jesus ask him, ' Lovest thou Me ? ' " [1]) : most
regard it as a free invention. [2] In these hypotheses
it is the imagination of the critics, not that of the
Evangelist, that is active. It is enough here to
oppose to them, conflicting and mutually destructive
in themselves, the direct and satisfying testimony
of the disciple who was *there*. It is, no doubt, a
miracle that is recorded—one of the " providential "
order—but the resemblance with that in St. Luke
begins and ends with the fact that it is a draught
of fishes. Circumstances and connexion are totally
different. In a symbolical respect it may well have
been designed as a reminder and renewal of the call
originally given, and a confirmation, suitable to
this period of new commissions, of the pledge which
accompanied that call · " From henceforth thou
shalt catch men."[3]

Noteworthy in this narrative, as in the preceding,
is the combination in Christ's Resurrection body
of seemingly opposite characters ; on the one hand,
mysterious (supernatural) traits, veiling recognition, and exciting awe in the beholders ; on the
other, attributes and functions which attest its full

---

[1] *Les Apôtres*, pp. 33–34.
[2] Keim takes this view of the whole chapter (*Jesus of
Nazara*, vi. pp. 314–18).
[3] Luke v. 10.

physical reality, and identity with the body that was crucified.

4. Chief among the appearances of Jesus after His Resurrection is unquestionably to be ranked the great meeting *on the mountain in Galilee*, of which St. Matthew alone preserves the record. [1] St. Matthew's testimony, however, is not wholly without corroboration. It is commonly assumed that St. Mark also had intended to give some account of this meeting, [2] which is usually, and no doubt correctly, identified with the appearance which St. Paul mentions " to above ¦five hundred brethren at once, of whom the greater part remain until now." [3] St. Matthew, indeed, speaks only of " the eleven disciples " in connexion with the meeting. He does so because it is with the Commission to the Apostles he is specially concerned. But the wider scope of the gathering is already evident in his own intimations regarding it. The meeting had been in view from the day of Resurrection. The summons to it was addressed to the " disciples," [4] who are by no means to be confined to the Apostles. The place and, we must suppose, the time also, had been definitely " appointed." [5]   It was to be in " a mountain " in Galilee—a place suitable for a

[1] Matt. xxviii. 16–20.
[2] Cf. Mark xvi. 7.   [3] 1 Cor. xv. 6.
[4] Matt. xxviii. 7, 9.   In ver. 10, "brethren."
[5] Ver. 16.   On whole incident, cf. Latham, *ut supra*, pp. 280–94.

general gathering. The intention, in short, was a collective meeting of disciples.

To this place, accordingly, at the appointed time, the Apostles and other disciples repaired and there, faithful to His promise, Jesus appeared to them. The expression " when they saw Him " [1] suggests some sudden appearance, while the clause " came unto them," [2] in the succeeding verse, points to approach from some little distance. In so large a company susceptibility would vary, and it is not surprising that it is on record that, when Jesus was first seen, " they worshipped Him, *but some doubted.*" [3]   The statement is a testimony to the genuineness of the narrative ; it is also an indirect indication of the presence of others. [4]   In the small body of the eleven there is hardly room for a " some." Whatever doubt there was would vanish when the Lord drew near and spoke.

With such a view of the Galilean meeting, objections to the genuineness of the great Commission, " Go ye, therefore, and make disciples of all the nations," etc., lose most of their force. Based as it is on the august declaration, " All authority hath been given unto Me in heaven and on earth," and culminating in the promise, " Lo, I am with you always, even unto the end of the world," [5] the

[1] Ver. 17.   [2] Ver. 18.   [3] Ibid.
[4] Cf. Latham, pp. 291–3 ; Allen, *St. Matthew*, pp. 303, 305.
[5] Cf. Latham, pp. 282–6 ; Allen, pp. 306–7.

Commission will be felt by most to hold its proper place.   If Jesus really rose, these, or words like these, are precisely what He might be expected to use on such an occasion.   Doubt of the words, as a rule goes along with doubt of the Resurrection itself.[1]

[The appearance to St. James[2] was dealt with in last chapter.]

5. Shortly after the great meeting in Galilee, the Apostles returned again to Jerusalem—from this time on, as every one admits, the continuous scene of their residence and labours.   The fact that they did return is confirmatory evidence that some decisive experience had awaited them in the north. A link, however, is still wanting to connect previous events with the waiting for Pentecost, and the bold action immediately thereafter taken in the founding of the Church.   That link is found in *the last appearance of the Lord to the Apostles*—the appearance alluded to by St. Paul in the words, " then, to all the Apostles "[3] and more circumstantially narrated by St. Luke, who brings it into direct

[1] The critical questions in this section are chiefly two : (1) Whether St. Matthew here follows the lost ending of St. Mark (some, as Allen, favour ; others doubt or deny) ; and (2) whether the words, " Baptizing them into the name," etc., should be omitted (after Eusebius). Prof. Lake says : " The balance of argument is in favour of the Eusebian text " (p. 88). Against this another sentence of his own may be quoted : " The text is found in all MSS. and versions " (p. 87).

[2] 1 Cor. xv. 7.   [3] Ibid.

relation with the Ascension [1] A difficulty is found
here in the fact that in his Gospel (chap. xxiv.) St.
Luke proceeds without break from Christ's first appearance to " the eleven " to His last words about
" the promise of the Father " and the Ascension at
Bethany ; whereas in Acts i. he interposes " forty
days " between the Resurrection and Ascension,
and assumes appearances of Christ spread over the
whole period.   Not only Strauss, Keim, Weizsäcker,
etc., but also Meyer, and many other critics, em-
phasize this " contradiction."   It may reasonably
be suspected, however, that " contradiction " occurring in books by the same writer, addressed to the
same person, one of which is formally a continuation
of the other, has its origin, less in fault of the author,
than in the failure of the critics to do justice to his
method.   St. Luke, in his second work, betrays
no consciousness of " contradiction " with his
first, and his acquaintance with St. Paul, and knowledge of the list of appearances in 1 Corinthians,[2]
make it, as formerly urged, unthinkable that he
should have supposed all the events between the
Resurrection and Ascension to be crowded into a
single day.   Neither, as a more careful inspection
of his narrative in the Gospel shows, does he suppose
this.   The sequence of events in chap, xxiv. makes

---

[1] Luke xxiv. 44–53 ; Acts i. 5–12.

[2] Weizsäcker thinks that St. Luke's mention of the
appearance of St. Peter " depended on the writer's acquaintance with the passage in Paul " (*Apost. Age*, ii. p. 11).

it clear that it was already late in the evening when Jesus appeared to "the eleven."[1] A meal followed. After this, if all happened on the same evening, there took place a lengthened exposition of the prophetic Scriptures. The disciples were then led out of Bethany, a mile and a half from the city. There they witnessed the Ascension. Afterwards they returned to Jerusalem "with great joy," and were continually in the Temple. Is it not self-evident that there is compressed into these closing verses of the Gospel far more than the events of one day?[2] Conscious of his purpose to write a fuller account of the circumstances of the Lord's parting with His disciples, the Evangelist foreshortens and summarizes his narrative of the instructions and promises which had their beginning at that first meeting, and were continued later.[3] Similarly, the citation of Christ's words in the closing verses of the Appendix to St. Mark must be regarded as a summary.

The last meeting of Christ with His Apostles took

---

[1] The disciples had returned from Emmaus after an evening meal there.

[2] Latham justly says : " I will not listen to the supposition that the events of Luke xxiv. 36–53 all happened in the one evening—this would make the Ascension take place in the dead of night " (p. 155).

[3] Cf. Godet, *St. Luke*, ii. p. 358 ; Plummer, *St. Luke*, pp. 561, 564. Luthardt says : " Luke draws into one the entire time from the day of the Resurrection to the Ascension " (*St. John*, iii. p. 356).

place, as we definitely learn from Acts i. 4, when
He was " assembled together with them " at Jerusalem. It was then His final instructions were given.
Even here the scene changes insensibly to Olivet,
where the Ascension is located. Jesus might have
simply " vanished " from the sight of His disciples,
as on previous occasions, but it was His will to leave
them in a way which would visibly mark the final
close of His temporal association with them. He
was " taken up," and " a cloud received Him out
of their sight." [1] As they stood, still gazing at the
spot where He had disappeared, angels, described
as " two men in white apparel " (if ever angels
were in place, it surely was at the Resurrection
and Ascension), admonished them that, as they
had seen Him depart, so in like manner He
would come again. The visible Ascension has its
counterpart in the visible Return.

It is the same picture of the Ascension, essentially, which is given in the close of St. Luke's
Gospel : " He parted from them, and was carried
up into heaven." [2] It matters little for the sense
whether the last clause is retained, as probably
it should be, or, with some authorities, is rejected, for
the context plainly shows the kind of " parting "
that is intended (cf. " received up," $\dot{\alpha}\nu\alpha\lambda\dot{\eta}\mu\psi\epsilon\omega\varsigma$, in
chap. ix. 51). The Appendix to St. Mark, likewise,
correctly gives the meaning :   " He was received up

_____
[1] Acts i. 10, 11.   [2] Luke xxiv. 51.

($\dot{a}\nu\epsilon\lambda\dot{\eta}\mu\phi\theta\eta$) into heaven, and sat down at the right hand of God." [1] Not in these passages only, but thro ghout the whole of the New Testament, it is implied that Jesus after His Resurrection " passed into the heavens," was exalted and glorified. [2]

The facts are now before us. It remains, as far as it can be reverently done, to sum up the *results* as to the nature of the body of the Lord during this transitional period between Resurrection and Ascension, and to consider briefly the problems which these raise. This, with the full recognition that, in the present state of knowledge, these problems are, in large part, necessarily insoluble.

[1] Mark xvi. 19.

[2] John vi. 62, xx. 17 ; Eph. iv. 8–10 ; 1 Tim. iii. 16 ; Heb. iv. 14 ; 1 Pet. iii. 21, 22, etc. On the Ascension cf. Godet, *St. Luke*, iii. pp. 367–71 ; Latham, chap. xii. Only a word need be said on the objection urged from Strauss down that the Ascension is confuted by its connexion with a now exploded cosmogony. A recent writer, Prof. A. O. Lovejoy, states the objection thus in *The Hibbert Journal*, April 1908, p. 503 : "This story [of the Resurrection] is inextricably involved with, and is unintelligible apart from, the complementary story of the Ascension, with its crude scene of levitation ; and this, in turn, is meaningless without the scheme of cosmic topography that places a heaven somewhere in space in a direction perpendicular to the earth's surface at the latitude and longitude of Bethany." The objection really rests on a crudely realistic view of the world of space and time, as if this was not itself the index and symbol of another and (to us) invisible world, to which a higher reality belongs (in illustration, cf. Stewart and Tait's *The Unseen Universe*). Reception into this world is not by way of spatial transition.

"I am not yet ascended" . . . "I ascend."[1] In these two parts of the one saying of Jesus the mystery of the Resurrection body is comprised.

On *earth*, as the history shows, Jesus had a body in all natural respects, corruptibility excepted, like our own. He hungered, He thirsted, He was weary, He suffered, He died of exhaustion and wounds. In *heaven*, that body has undergone transformation; has become "the body of His glory."[2] In comparison with the natural, it has become a spiritual— "a pneumatic"—body, assimilated to, and entirely under the control of, the spiritual nature and forces that reside in it and work through it. In the interval between the Resurrection and the Ascension its condition must be thought of as *intermediate* between these two states—no longer merely natural (the act of Resurrection itself proclaimed this), yet not fully entered into the state of glorification. It presents characters, requisite for the proof of its identity, which show that the earthly condition is still not wholly parted with. It discovers qualities and powers which reveal that the supra-terrestrial condition is already begun. The apparently inconsistent aspects, therefore, under which Christ's body appears in the narratives do not constitute a bar to the acceptance of the truthfulness of the accounts; they may rather, in their congruity with what is to be

---

[1] John xx. 17.　　　　[2] Phil. iii. 21.

looked for in the Risen One, who has shown His power over death, but has not yet entered into His glory, be held to furnish a mark of credibility. How unlikely that the myth-forming spirit—not to say the crudeness of invention—should be able to seize so exactly the two-fold aspect which the manifestation of the Redeemer in His triumph over the grave must necessarily present!

Let these peculiarities of the Lord's Risen body be a little more closely considered.

1. On the one side, the greatest pains are taken to prove that the body in which Jesus appeared was a *true body*—not a spirit or phantasm, but the veritable body which had suffered on the Cross, and been laid in the tomb. It could be seen, touched, handled. It bore on it the marks of the Passion. To leave no room for doubt of its reality, it is told that on at least two, probably on three, occasions, Jesus *ate* with His disciples. With this accords the fact that the grave in which the body of Jesus had been buried on the Friday evening was found empty on the Easter Sunday morning. It was seen before that it was undeniably the belief of St. Paul and of the whole Apostolic Church that Jesus rose on the third day in the very body which had been buried.[1]

---

[1] Ménégoz says : " The mention of the third day would have no sense if Paul had not accepted the belief of the community of Jerusalem that on the third day Jesus went

2. On the other hand, it is equally evident that the Resurrection body of Jesus was *not simply natural*. It had attributes proclaiming its connexion with that supra-terrestrial sphere to which it now more properly belonged. These attributes, moreover, however difficult to reconcile with the more tangible properties, can still not be regarded as mere legendary embellishments, for they appear in some degree in all the presentations.

The peculiarities chiefly calling for notice in this respect are the following :—

(1) There is the mysterious power which Jesus seems to have possessed of withdrawing Himself in greater or less degree from the *recognition* of those around Him. In more than one of the narratives, as has been seen, it is implied that there was something strange—something unfamiliar or mysterious —in His aspect, which prevented His immediate recognition even by those intimate with Him ; which held them in awe ; while again, when some gesture, word, or look, revealed to them suddenly who He was, they were surprised, as the truth flashed upon them, that they had not recognized Him sooner.

The instances which come under this head, indeed, differ in character. It is possible that the failure of Mary Magdalene to recognize Jesus at the begin-

forth alive from the tomb " (*La Péché et la Redemption d'apres S. Paul*, p. 261 ; quoted by Bruce).

ning [1] may have been due to her absorption in her grief; but it was probably in part occasioned also by some alteration in His appearance. It is said of the Emmaus disciples that "their eyes were holden that they should not know Him," [2] elsewhere that He appeared to them "in another form." [3] The former expression need not, perhaps, be pressed to imply a supernatural action on their senses. It may mean simply that they did not know Him; that there was that about Him which prevented recognition. Yet when He was revealed to them in the breaking of bread, they appear to have marvelled at their blindness in not discerning Him sooner. In the incident at the Sea of Tiberias, the disciples may have been hindered from recognizing Jesus by the distance or the dimness of the dawn. The narrative, nevertheless, implies something in Christ's aspect which awed and restrained them, so that, even when they knew Him, they did not ask, "Who art Thou?" [4]

(2) It is an extension of the same supernatural quality when the power is attributed to Jesus of withdrawing Himself from *sensible perception* altogether. At Emmaus, we are told, "He vanished out of their sight." [5] On other occasions He appeared and disappeared. [6] Here, apparently, is an emerging from, and withdrawing into, complete invisibility.

---

[1] John xx. 14.   [2] Luke xxiv. 16.   [3] Mark xvi. 12.
[4] John xxi. 12.   [5] Luke xxiv. 31.
[6] Luke xxiv. 36; John xx. 19, 26.

(3) The climax in supernatural quality is reached when Jesus is represented as withdrawing Himself wholly from conditions of space and time, and as *transcending physical limitations*—in appearing, e.g., to His disciples within closed doors,[1] or being found in different places at short intervals, or, finally, in ascending from earth to heaven in visible form.[2] A body in which powers like these are manifested is on the point of escaping from earthly conditions altogether—as, in truth, the body of Jesus was.

Little help can be gained from natural analogies in throwing light on properties so mysterious as those now described, or in removing the feeling of incredulity with which they must always be regarded by minds that persist in applying to them only the standards of ordinary experience. Daily, indeed, are men being forced to recognize that the world holds more mysteries than they formerly imagined it to do. Probably physicists are not so sure of the absolute impenetrability of matter,[3] or even of the conservation of energy, as they once were ; and newer speculations on the etheric basis of matter, and on the relation of the seen to an unseen universe (or universes), with forces and laws largely un-

---

[1] Luke xxiv. 36 ; John xx. 19, 26.
[2] Luke xxiv. 51 ; Acts i. 9. On the Ascension, see note above, p. 195.
[3] Cf. Stallo's *Concepts of Modern Physics* (Inter. Scien. Lib.), pp. 91 2, 178–82,

known,[1] open up vistas of possibility which may hold in them the key to phenomena even as extraordinary as those in question.   In another direction, Mr. R. J. Campbell finds himself able to accept the physical Resurrection, and " the mysterious appearances and disappearances of the body of Jesus," on the ground of a theory of a " three-dimensional " and " four-dimensional " world,[2] which probably will be incomprehensible to most.   Then the Society of Psychical Research has its experiments to prove a direct control of matter by spirit in extraordinary, if not preternatural, ways.[3]   Such considerations may aid in removing prejudices, but they do little really to explain the remarkable phenomena of the bodily manifestations of Jesus to His disciples. These must still rest on their connexion with His unique Person.

Specially suggestive in this last relation are the indications in the Gospels themselves that, even during His earthly ministry, Christ's body possessed powers and obeyed laws higher than those to which ordinary humanity is subject.   Two of the best attested incidents in the cycle of Gospel tradition —His Walking on the Sea,[4] and the Transfigura-

[1] Cf. *The Unseen Universe* (Stewart and Tait), pp. 166, 189–90.

[2] *The New Theology*, pp. 220–24.

[3] Cf. Myers, *Human Personality*, ii. pp. 204 ff. ; Sir Oliver Lodge, *Hibbert Journal*, April, 1908, pp. 574 ff.

[4] Matt. xiv. 22–33 ;   Mark vi. 45–52 ;   John vi. 15–21. In St. Matthew's narrative St. Peter also shared this power till his faith failed.

tion [1]—will occur as examples. Mighty powers worked in Him which already suggested to Herod One risen from the dead ; [2] powers which might be expected to manifest themselves in a higher degree when He actually did rise.

[1] Matt. xvii. 1–8 ; Mark ix. 2–8 ; Luke ix. 28–36. Wellhausen (*Das Evang. Marci,* pp. 75–6) actually supposes that the Transfiguration was originally an appearance of the Risen Christ to St. Peter. Loisy follows him in the conjecture (ii. p. 39).

[2] Matt. xiv. 2.

THE APOSTOLIC CHURCH—VISIONAL
AND APPARITIONAL THEORIES

VIII

THE APOSTOLIC CHURCH—VISIONAL AND APPARITIONAL THEORIES

IT has been seen that the facts of the historical witness for the Resurrection form a chain of evidence extending from the empty grave on the morning of the third day and the message of the women, through the successive appearances of Jesus in Jerusalem and Galilee, till the day that He was finally " taken up "[1] into heaven in the view of His disciples. On these facts was based, in the immediate witnesses, the firm conviction, which nothing could shake, that their Lord, who had been crucified, had risen from the dead, and had been exalted to heavenly dominion. Their testimony, held fast to under the severest trial of privation, suffering, and death, was public, and no attempt was ever made, so far as is known, to refute their assertion. The effects of the faith in the first disciples, and in the hearts and lives of their converts, were of a nature to establish that they were the

[1] Acts i. 2.

victims of no illusion ; that they built on rock, not sand.

For this is the point next to be observed : the historical evidence for the Resurrection of Jesus is not all the evidence. As the Resurrection had its antecedents in the history and claims of Jesus, so it had its *results*. Pentecost is such a result. The Apostolic Church is such a result. The conversion of St. Paul, the Epistles of the New Testament, the Spirit-filled lives of a multitude of believers are such results. The Church founded on the Apostolic witness has endured for nineteen centuries. Christian experience throughout all these ages is a fact which only a Living Christ can explain or sustain. The Apostle speaks of the " power " of Christ's Resurrection.[1] That which continuously exerts " power " is a demonstrable reality.

There is space only for a glance at one or two of these results in the Apostolic Age.

1. The *Day of Pentecost*, in the Book of Acts, is the *sequel* to the Resurrection and Ascension. " Being, therefore," said St. Peter, " by the right hand of God exalted, and having received of the Father the promise of the Holy Spirit, He hath poured forth this, which ye do see and hear." [2] The cavils which have been raised against the general historicity of the first chapters of the Acts,

---

[1] Phil. iii. 10.   [2] Acts ii. 33.

which narrate the outpouring of the Spirit, and the origin of the Church at Jerusalem,[1] are met, apart from the note of clear remembrance and full information in the narrative itself, by one single consideration. It is as incredible that the Mother of all the Churches—the undoubted seat of Apostolic residence and activity for many years—should have been unaware of, or have forgotten, the circumstances of its own origin, as that, say, Germany should forget its Reformation by Luther, or America its Declaration of Independence.

2. The crucial fact of *St. Paul's conversion* took place at most five or six years after the Resurrection.[2] It happened, therefore, when the original witnesses were still alive and located at Jerusalem, and when remembrance had as yet no time to grow obscure, or tradition to become corrupted or perverted. Three years later St. Paul lodged for a fortnight with St. Peter [3]—chief of the Apostles —at Jerusalem, and there also met James, the Lord's brother. Then, if not before, he must have made himself familiar with the chief details of the Jerusalem tradition regarding Christ's death and Resurrection. Earlier, while yet a persecutor, he

---

[1] Even Harnack, who partly shares in the objection, admits that " the instances of alleged incredibility have been much exaggerated by critics " (*Lukas der Arzt*, p. 88).

[2] The dates range from 31–2 A.D. (Harnack), 33 (Ramsay), 35–6 (Conybeare and Howson, Turner).

[3] Gal. i. 18.

had shared in the martyrdom of that precursor of his own, St. Stephen, who, in dying, had the vision of Jesus in heaven waiting to receive his departing spirit.[1]

No fewer than three times in the Book of Acts the circumstances of St. Paul's vision of Jesus on the way to Damascus are narrated,[2] and it can scarcely be doubted by any one who accepts St. Luke's authorship of the Book that the information which these accounts contain was derived originally from St. Paul's own lips.[3] This, again, alone should suffice to set aside the contradiction which some have imagined between the Apostle's own conception of his conversion and the narratives in Acts, as well as the charge of vital contradictions in the narratives themselves.[4] As penned by the same writer, in the compass of the same work, the accounts must, in all reason, be supposed to be in harmony with each other to the author's own thought, whatever critics may now choose to make of them.

[1] Acts vii. 51–60.

[2] Acts. ix. 1–22 ; xxii. 1–16 ; xxvi. 1–18.

[3] The first is St. Luke's narrative ; the second is in St. Paul's defence before Lysias, when St. Luke was probably present (a " we " section) ; the third is in St. Paul's defence before Agrippa, when St. Luke again was probably present.

[4] Particulars given in one narrative and not in another are not contradictions. The writer being the same, the particulars must in each case have been known to him, though not expressed.

It is not necessary to discuss at length the reality and objectivity of this appearance of the glorified Jesus to Saul the persecutor, when his mad rage against the saints was in full career. The sudden and revolutionary change then wrought, with its lasting moral and spiritual effects, is one which no " kicking against the goods " [1] in Saul's conscience, or " explosion " of forces of the subliminal consciousness which had been silently gathering to a head, can satisfactorily explain. Objective elements are implied in the great light, " above the brightness of the sun," that suddenly shone around the whole company, causing all, as the longer narrative shows, to fall to the ground, and in the voice which all heard, though Saul alone apprehended its articulate purport. [2] It is not so clear whether Saul not simply heard the Lord speak, [3] but beheld His form in the heavenly glory. That the latter, really, was the case, is suggested by the contrast in the words used of his companions, " hearing the voice, but beholding no man," [4] and by the words of St. Paul himself, " Have I not seen Jesus our Lord ? " [5] Most certain it is that St. Paul himself was absolutely convinced, both at the time of the vision and ever after, of the reality of

[1] Acts. xxvi. 14.

[2] Cf. Acts ix. 3, 7 ; xxvi. 13, 14.

[3] Weizsäcker and Loisy urge that St. Paul only saw a light and heard words.

[4] Acts ix. 7.   [5] 1 Cor. ix. 1.

Christ's appearance to him, and of the call he then received to be the Apostle of the Gentiles. Accordiugly, he confidently ranks the appearance to himself with those to the other Apostles.[1] With the outward vision went an inward revelation of God's Son to his soul [2]—outward and inward com. bining to effect an entire transformation in his conceptions of God, man, Christ, the world : everything.[3] This was the turning-point in St. Paul's history ; a turning-point, also, in the history of Christianity. Before, Christ's enemy, he was now Christ's devoted " slave " (δοῦλος) and Apostle. The Spirit that thenceforward wrought in him with mightiest results was the surest attestation of the genuineness of his experience.

3. In the prominence naturally given to the testimony of St. Paul, it should not be overlooked how pervasive is the witness of the *entire New Testament* to this same great primary fact of the Lord's Resurrection.   It was seen that St. Peter was one of the first to whom Jesus appeared. But St. Peter has left an Epistle (the question of the second Epistle may here be waived), which rings throughout with the joyful hope and confidence begotten by the Resurrection of Jesus from the dead.[4] Jesus appeared to St. James ; and St.

---

[1] I Cor. xv. 8.   [2] Gal. i. 15, 16.   [3] Cf. 2 Cor. v. 16.
[4] I Pet. i. 3, 21 ; iii. 21, 22

James has likewise an Epistle which extols Jesus as " the Lord of glory," and looks for His coming as nigh at hand.[1] St. John also, in Gospel, Epistle, and Apocalypse, presupposes or declares the Resurrection. The hope he holds out to believers is that, when He—Jesus—shall be " manifested," they shall be like Him, for they shall see Him even as He is.[2]

The historical attestation of the Resurrection in the New Testament has now been examined, and, so far as the inquiry has gone, the Resurrection of Jesus, as the foundation of the faith, hope, and life of the Church, stands fast. But the question will still be pressed—Is there no alternative conclusion? Is it not possible that the facts which appear to render support to the belief in the Resurrection in the Apostolic Age may be explained in another way? It has already been seen that this is the contention of a large class of writers in our own day. It has also been made apparent that there is as yet little approach to agreement among them in the rival theories they advance to supplant the Apostolic belief. The study of these " modern " theories may, indeed, well be ranked as a supplementary chapter in the exhibition of the positive evidence for the Resurrection. It is in this corroborative light it is proposed here principally to regard them.

[1] Jas. ii. 1 ; v. 7–9.   [2] John iii. 2.

The two main pillars of belief in the Resurrection were found to be the empty tomb on the morning of the third day, and the actual appearances of the Risen Lord to His disciples.

1. Some light has already been cast on the various expedients by which it is attempted in the newer theories to get rid of the fact of *the empty tomb.* Either, as by not a few, the story is treated as un-historical,[1] and roundabout attempts are made to explain its origin by inference from the (visionary) appearances to the disciples in Galilee ; or, grant-ing a basis of fact in the narratives, it is conjectured that the body of Jesus had been secretly removed from the tomb, and disposed of elsewhere ; or, as by Professor Lake, it is supposed that the women made a mistake in the tomb which they visited. These curiosities of theory need not be further dwelt upon. Christian people to whom they are offered may be excused for echoing the lament of Mary Magdalene : " They have taken away my Lord, and I know not where they have laid Him."[2] For the critics do not even profess to know where the body of Jesus was put. The disciples, indeed, are now usually exonerated from participation in a deliberate fraud, and speculation varies between Pilate, the Sanhedrim, and Joseph of Arimathæa

---

[1] " An empty grave was never seen by any disciple of Jesus " (A. Meyer, p. 213).

[2] John xx. 11.

as persons who may have removed the body. Others, more wisely, leave the matter in the vagueness of ignorance.[1] There remains the fact which cannot be got over—a fact fatal to all this arbitrary theorising—that within a few weeks at most of the Crucifixion, at Pentecost and in the days immediately thereafter—the disciples, raised from despair to a joyful confidence which nothing could destroy, were, as already told, boldly and publicly proclaiming in the streets of the very city where Jesus had been crucified that He was risen from the dead; were maintaining the same testimony before the tribunals; were stirring the city, and making thousands of converts. Yet not the least attempt was made, either by the rulers, or by any one else interested, to stay the movement, and silence the preachers, as might easily have been done, had their testimony been false, by pointing to where the body of Jesus still lay, or by showing how it had come to be removed from the tomb in which it had, after the Crucifixion, to the knowledge of all, been deposited. *Did not* in this case spells *could not*, and the empty tomb remains an unim-

---

[1] Thus Renan; now also Loisy. The latter says: " It appears useless to discuss here the different hypotheses regarding the removal of the body [assumed by the critic to be a fact], whether by Joseph of Arimathæa, or by the proprietor of the tomb, or by the orders of the Sanhedrim, or by Mary of Bethany, or by the Apostles there " (*Les Évangiles Synoptiques*, ii. p. 720).

peachable witness to the truth of the message that
the Lord had risen.

2. If the empty tomb cannot be got rid of, may
it not at least be possible to show that *the appearances of Jesus* can be explained on another hypothesis than that of a physical Resurrection—either
by subjective hallucinations, which is the older
form of the visional theory, or, if that be thought
inadequate, by real apparitions of the (spiritually)
risen Christ, which is the form of theory now pre-
ferred by many ?   The aim in both of these classes
of theories, is to relieve the mind from the difficulty of believing in an actual rising of the body
from the grave ; in other words, to do away with
the physical miracle. Only, while the purely•
visional theory takes away all ground for belief in
the Resurrection, the other, or apparitional, by
substituting a spiritual rising for the corporeal,
and allowing real manifestations of the Risen Jesus,
proposes in a certain way to conserve that belief.
Is this admissible ?   It is hoped that a brief exam-
nation will make clear how far either theory is
from furnishing a tenable explanation of the facts
it has to deal with.

(1) Attention has to be called, first, to an interesting fact which has already been repeatedly alluded
to in the course of these discussions.   It is to be observed with regard to most of these modern visional
and apparitional theories that, in complete break

with tradition, they feel the necessity of *transferring the appearances of Jesus from Jerusalem*, where the earlier of them are related to have happened *to the more remote region of Galilee*, and so of dissociating them wholly from the message of the women at the tomb.[1] A slight qualification of this is that some are disposed to see in St. Luke's narrative of the appearance at Emmaus a reminiscence of appearances in the *neighbourhood* of Jerusalem.[2] But the greater appearances—all those included in the list of St. Paul in 1 Corinthians xv. 3–8—are transported without further ado to Galilee.

The advantage of this change of *locale* for the theory is obvious. It separates the visions from the events of the Easter morning, gives time for visions to develop, transfers them to scenes where memory and imagination may be supposed to be more prepared to work, frees them from the control of the hard realities of the situation. As Strauss puts it: "If the transference of the appearances to Galilee disengages us from the third day as the period of the commencement of them, the longer time thus gained makes the reaction in the minds of the disciples more conceivable."[3]

The real course of events after the Crucifixion

[1] Thus Strauss, Keim, Weizsäcker, Pfleiderer, Harnack, O. Holtzmann, Lake, Loisy, etc.

[2] Thus A. Meyer (pp. 134, 136); Lake (pp. 218–19).

[3] *New Life of Jesus*, i. p. 437.

is alleged to be unmistakably indicated by the statement of the Evangelists · " They [the disciples] all left Him and fled " (whither should they flee but to their old home ?), supported as this is by the words of Jesus : " It is written, I will smite the shepherd," etc., which He expressly connects with His going before them into Galilee ; [1] and again by the fact that St. Mark and St. Matthew point to Galilee as the place of Christ's meeting with His disciples.[2] It is true that St. Luke and St. John—in part also St. Matthew—locate the first appearances in Jerusalem ; but this representation, declared to be irreconcilable with the other, is promptly set aside as unhistorical.[3] Internal probability is likewise claimed in favour of Galilee.[4] To Galilee, therefore, without hesitation, all the leading appearances of Jesus—the appearance to St. Peter, the appearances to the Apostles, to the five hundred, to St. James, etc.—are carried.[5]

[1] Matt. xxvi. 31, 32, 56 ; Mark xiv. 27, 28, 50 ; John xvi. 32.

[2] Matt. xxviii. 7 ; Mark xvi. 7.

[3] " This last conception is irreconcilable with the first " (Strauss, i. p. 435). " Now these two representations are irreconcilable " (Weizsäcker, i. p. 2). " This is evidently not genuine but coloured history " (Keim, vi. p. 284).

[4] Strauss, i. pp. 436-7.

[5] Keim is emphatic : " These appearances of Jesus took place, according to the plainest evidence, in Galilee, not in Jerusalem " (p. 281). " Nothing can be plainer than that all the appearances are to be located in the mother country of Christianity " (p. 283).

It is not difficult to show that this hypothesis, directly opposed as it is to nine-tenths of the tradition we possess, has no real foothold even in the facts alleged in its support.[1] To give it any colour, it is necessary to get behind the tradition even in St. Mark, the supposed original, and in St. Matthew, and to reinterpret the *data* in a way fatal to the good sense and veracity of the narratives. There is nothing in St. Matthew, St. Mark, or St. John to countenance the idea that the " scattering " and " fleeing " of the disciples had reference to a flight into Galilee. On the very night of the " fleeing "[2] St. Peter is found in the High Priest's palace. The threefold denial into which he was there betrayed does not look like a purpose to go at once into Galilee. St. Matthew and St. Mark, again, who announce that Jesus will go before the disciples into Galilee, as plainly imply that the disciples to whom the message is sent are still in Jerusalem.[3] St. Matthew himself records an appearance in Jerusalem in which the same direction to go into Galilee is embodied.[4] St. John predicts the " scattering," [5] yet gives detailed accounts of the meetings

---

[1] For a criticism of the theory, cf. Loofs, *Die Auferstehungsberichte*, pp. 18–25. Loofs, however, is himself arbitrary in transferring *all* the appearances to Jerusalem.

[2] Matt. xxvi. 58 ; Mark xiv. 54.

[3] This is supposed to be an expedient to cover the earlier disgrace of the flight. Cf. Loofs in criticism (P. 20).

[4] Matt. xxviii. 9, 10.   [5] John xvi. 32.

in Jerusalem. It is not easy to see, therefore, how Keim can suppose that St. John's words " preserve the reminiscence that they [the disciples] fled towards their home, that is, towards Galilee." [1] St. Luke knew something of St. Paul's beliefs. He must have known something also of St. Paul's understanding of the locality of the appearances in I Corinthians xv. Yet he places the appearance to St. Peter in Jerusalem on the very day of the Resurrection.[2] And where is there the least evidence that St. Paul, who knew Jerusalem, but never mentions Galilee, intended all the appearances he enumerates to be located in that region ?

There *were* Galilean appearances. St. Matthew tells of one, St. Mark probably intended to tell of one, St. John tells of one. But how extremely unlikely, assuming the departure into Galilee to have been simply a chance scattering, that the eleven Apostles should be found on different occasions convened to receive visions ? Or that above five hundred brethren should be brought together in that region, without previous appointment, for a similar purpose ? Or that immediately afterwards Apostles and disciples should be found again at Jerusalem, a united body, animated by a common purpose and hope, and ready to testify at all hazards that Jesus had been raised *from the tomb* ?

---

[1] *Jesus of Nazara*, vi. p. 283.
[2] Luke xxiv. 34.

The theory of the transference of the earlier appearances to Galilee being discarded as one which a sound treatment of the sources cannot justify, the way is cleared for a judgment on the *visional* and *apparitional* theories which are put forward to explain the appearances themselves.

(2) The theory of *subjective visions*, or *mental hallucinations*, though its glaring weaknesses have often been exposed, by none more effectively than by Keim himself—is still the favourite with many.[1] Visions, under excitement, or in persons of a high-strung, nervous temperament, especially among ascetics, are an often-recurring phenomenon in religious history.[2] Visions, too, in an emotional atmosphere, are contagious. Here then, it may be thought, is a principle which can be invoked to furnish an easy and natural explanation of the abnormal experiences of the disciples

---

[1] It was the theory of Strauss and Renan, and is favoured by Weizsäcker, Harnack, A. Meyer, O. Holtzmann, Loisy, etc.

[2] See the long chapter of instances in A. Meyer, *Die Auferstehung Christi*, pp. 217-70. Cf. Keim, iv. pp. 346-8 : ": Thus, not to speak of the Old and New Testaments with their long lists of examples, Maximilla and the Montanists saw Christ, the Maid of Orleans received the Archangel Michael and S.S. Catherine and Margaret, Francis of Assisi saw the Lord as a seraph, and Savonarola looked upon both obscure and clear pictures of the future through the ordinary ministry of angels. In the same way, the eccentric Mohammed, the pious Swedenborg, the illuminated bookseller Nicolai, have had visions," etc. (p. 346).

after the Resurrection. From St. Paul's " vision " of Jesus on the way to Damascus, it is argued that the earlier appearances which he enumerates must have been visionary also.

The forms which the vision-theory assumes are legion. Renan's is the most naïve, idyllic, and fanciful. Renan has no difficulty with the appearances at Jerusalem. According to him, the minds of the disciples swam in a delicious intoxication almost from the hour of the Crucifixion. " Heroes do not die." [1] Their Master must rise again. It was Mary Magdalene who set the train of visions in motion.[2] In the garden she believed that she saw and heard Jesus.[3] Divine hallucination! Her enthusiasm gave to the world a resuscitated god![4] Others at once caught the infection.[5] The most trifling incidents—" a current of air, a creaking window, a casual murmur " [6]— sufficed to start a vision. St. Peter's vision (which St. Paul misunderstood) was really his glimpse of the white grave-clothes in the tomb.[7] The dis-

---

[1] *Les Apôtres*, p. 3. See above, p. 146.

[2] " Mary alone loved enough to dispense with nature, and to have revived the phantom of the perfect Master... The glory, then, of the Resurrection belongs to Mary Magdalene " (pp. 12, 13).

[3] " The vision gently receded, and said to her : ' Touch Me not ! ' Gradually the shadow disappeared " (p. 11).

[4] *Vie de Jésus*, p. 434 ; *Les Apôtres*, p. 13.

[5] Ibid., pp. 16, 17.   [6] P. 22.

[7] P. 12.

ciples at Emmaus, in their rapture, mistook the
" pious Jew " who had expounded to them the Scriptures for Jesus. Suddenly he had vanished ! [1]
A breath of wind made the disciples in the closed
room think they recognized Jesus. " It was impossible to doubt ; Jesus was present ; He was
there, in the assembly." [2] Visions multiplied on
every hand. [3] Sometimes, " during meal time,
Jesus was seen to appear, taking the bread, bles-
sing it, breaking it, and offering it." [4] When the
enthusiasm chilled, the disciples revived it by going
in a joyous company to Galilee. [5] There they had
new experiences. [6] It was all too lovely to last, so
by and by the excitement died away, and the visions
ceased ! [7]

The falsetto note in these descriptions is all too
obvious, and sober-minded advocates of the vision
hypothesis usually now take another, if hardly
more successful, line. Jerusalem, as has been seen,

[1] Pp. 20–1.   [2] P. 22.

[3] " Visions were multiplied without number " (P. 25).
There is not a word in the narratives to countenance this.

[4] P. 26.

[5] " In a melancholy mood, they thought of the lake
and of the beautiful mountains where they had received
a foretaste of the Kingdom of God. . The majority
of the disciples then departed, full of joy and hope, perhaps
in the company of the caravan, which took back the pil-
grims from the Feast of the Passover " (pp. 28, 29).

[6] " The visions, at first, on the lake appear to have
been pretty frequent " (p. 32). Again quite unhistorical.

[7] Pp. 45 fl.

is abandoned as too near the scene of events; the third day also is set aside as affording too little time for the recovery of the disciples from despair. But Galilee, whither the disciples are carried, with its memories and tender associations, revives hope, and brings back the image of the Master. One day, perhaps by the Lake of Galilee (a reminiscence is discerned in St. John xxi.[1]), St. Peter sees a bright light, or something of the kind, and fancies it is Jesus.[2] By a mysterious telepathy, his experience affects the remaining Apostles, who happen to be gathered together, and they also have visions. The contagion spreads, and on another occasion 500 brethren at once have visions. By and by the visions cease as suddenly as they began. Returning to Jerusalem, the Apostles are met by the women, and for the first time (thus Professor Lake, etc.) hear of the empty tomb. Their faith is confirmed, and the women are established by the visions in their conviction that Jesus is risen.

It will be seen, to begin with, that to gain for this visional theory any semblance of plausibility, every fact in the Gospel history has to be changed—time, place, nature of the events, mood of the disciples, etc.—while scenes, conditions, and experiences are invented of which the Gospels know nothing. It is not the facts on record that are

[1] Thus Harnack, Loisy, etc.
[2] Cf. Weizsäcker, A. Meyer, etc.

explained, but a different (imaginary) set of facts altogether. According to the history, the first appearances took place in Jerusalem on the very day of the Resurrection. They took place independently. There was no preparedness to see visions, but, on the contrary, deep depression and rooted incredulity, not removed till Jesus, by sensible tokens, put his corporeal reality beyond doubt. The appearances were not momentary glimpses, but, at least in several of the cases, prolonged interviews. They were not excited by every trifling circumstance, nor ceaselessly multiplied. They numbered only ten altogether, five of them on the first day. The subjects of them were not nervous, hysterical persons, but men of stolid, practical judgment, fishermen, a tax-gatherer like St. Matthew, a matter-of-fact, unideal man like St. Philip, a sceptic like St. Thomas. In no case is there the slightest trace of preparatory excitement. If, when Jesus appeared, the disciples were " affrighted," it was at the thought that a spirit appeared to them,[1] and this idea (a chance for the vision hypothesis) had to be dispelled before they would believe that it was Jesus. Ordinarily they were calm and collected. It is obvious that for the explanation of *such* appearances a vision theory is useless.

Even on its own ground, however, it must be held that the vision theory breaks down in the

---

[1] Luke xxiv. 37–8.

most essential points. It is not, for instance, the case that there is any general predisposition to believe in the resurrection of " heroes," or to affirm that heroes have actually risen. No single example can be produced of belief in the resurrection of an historical personage such as Jesus was : none at least on which anything was ever founded. What *is* found is an unwillingness to believe, or to admit, in certain cases,[1] for a time, that the hero is really dead. The Christian Resurrection is thus a fact without historical analogy. There was, moreover, nothing in the nature of visions, assuming that the disciples had them, to give rise to the idea of a *bodily* Resurrection. " Visions " are phantasmal, and would be construed as " apparitions " of the dead, not as proofs of resurrection.[2] This is precisely what the Apostles at first did think about the appearances of Jesus. Lastly, as checking a purely visional theory, there is the immovable fact of the empty tomb. It would, indeed, be an extraordinary coincidence if, in the environs of Jerusalem, the tomb of Jesus was found empty, while, without previous knowledge of a Resurrection, the disciples began in Galilee to have visions of a Risen Lord !

---

[1] The cases are not numerous ; that of Mohammed, which Renan cites, is not really one. Mohammed's death was never really doubted.

[2] Cf. B. Weiss, *Life of Christ*, iii. p. 390 (E. T.).

Psychologically, no good cause has ever been shown why the disciples should have this marvellous outburst of visionary experience; should have it so early as the third day, should have it simultaneously, should have it within a strictly limited period, after which the visions as suddenly ceased, should never afterwards waver or doubt about it, should be inspired by it for the noblest work ever done on earth.[1] If anything is certain historically, it is that the death of their Master plunged the disciples into deepest despondency, that their hearts, always " slow to believe," were sad, and their hopes broken, and that, so far from expecting a Resurrection, they could hardly be persuaded of the fact even after it occurred. Even the words which Jesus had spoken on the subject had not been apprehended in a sense which helped them to believe. The women who visited the tomb had assuredly no expectation of finding the Lord risen. Even had their faith been stronger than it was, that would not have caused the appearances.

Equally unaccountable on a purely visional theory is the *outcome* of belief in the Resurrection. It was this consideration which weighed most of all with Keim, whose view is thus summed up by Godet: " It would be difficult to understand how,

[1] Keim forcibly urges against the vision-theory the orderly, regular character and early cessation of the appearances (vi. pp. 356–7). Cf. also Beyschlag, *Leben Jesu*, i. pp. 430–50.

from a society held together by over-excitement, issuing in visions, could have proceeded the Christian Church, with its lucidity of thought and earnestness of moral activity." [1] The visions not only cease, but as Keim points out, make way for a diametrically opposite mental current. From enthusiastic excitement, the impetus of which would have gone on working, as in Montanism, for a long period, there is a sudden transition to self-possession and clear-mindedness " If therefore," Keim argues, " there was actually an early, an immediate transition from the visions to a calm self-possession, and to a self-possessed energy, then the visions did not proceed from self-generated visionary over-excitement and fanatical agitation among the multitude." [2]

(3) Impressed by these difficulties, it is not surprising to find a tendency exhibiting itself among recent writers to concede the inadequacy of a purely subjective account of the appearances to the disciples, and to fall back on a theory of spiritual yet *real* manifestations of the Risen Christ—on what is called above an *apparitional* theory. Keim is not the earliest, but he is one of the best known representatives of this theory,[3] which is now thought by certain " moderns " to receive support from the

---

[1] Godet, *Defence of the Christian Faith*, p. 88.
[2] Keim, vi. pp. 357–8. Cf. Weiss, *ut supra*, iii. p. 387.
[3] *Ut supra*, vi. pp. 361–5.

evidence collected by the Society of Psychical Research on apparitions of the dead, or phantasms of persons at the time of death.[1] The view is one which commends itself to prominent Ritschlians, e.g. to Johannes Weiss.[2] It is put forward as probable by Professor Lake.[3] Keim thinks that in this way he saves the truth of the Resurrection (" thus, though much has fallen away, the secure faith-fortress of the Resurrection remains.")[4]

Keim's theory, in brief, is that, while the body of the Crucified Jesus slept on in the tomb in which it had received " honourable burial,"[5] His spirit manifested itself by supernatural impressions on the minds of the disciples—what he calls " telegrams from heaven "[6]—giving them the assurance that He still lived, and grounding a firm hope of immortality. Keim will not even refuse to those who may require it the belief that the vision took the form of " corporeal appearances."[7] The newer theories rely more on the evidence of apparitions to bring the appearances of Jesus within the scope of natural law—the idea of " law " being widened to take in psychical manifestations from the unseen world.[8] So far from belief in immortality being

---

[1] Cf. Lake, *Resur. of Jesus Christ*, pp. 271-6; Myers, *Human Personality*, i. p. 288.

[2] *Das Nachfolge Christi*, pp. 99, 151.

[3] *Ut supra.*   [4] P. 365.   [5] P. 271.   [6] Pp. 364-5.

[7] P. 362.

[8] Cf. Prof. Lake, m agreement with Dr. Rashdall : " A

based on the Resurrection, Professor Lake, in a passage earlier quoted, would seem to say that this belief (including the survival of Christ's personality) must remain an hypothesis till experts have sifted the evidence for the alleged psychical manifestations.[1]

It is not necessary here to investigate the degree of truth which belongs to the class of phenomena with which psychical research deals, or to discuss the alternative explanations which may be given of such phenomena. There is no call to deny the reality of telepathic communication between living minds, or the possibility of impressions being conveyed from one mind to another in the hour of death. The whole region is obscure, and needs further exploration. ' What it is necessary to insist upon is that nothing of the kind answers to the proper Scriptural idea of Resurrection, and that it is a mistake, involving a real yielding up of the Christian basis, to rest the proof of Christ's rising from the dead in any degree on *data* so elusive,

real though supernormal psychological event, but which involved nothing which can properly be spoken of as a suspension of natural law " (p. 269 ; cf. p. 277).

[1] " It remains merely an hypothesis until it can be shown that personal life does endure beyond death, is neither extinguished nor suspended, and is capable of manifesting its existence to us . . . but we must wait until the experts have sufficiently sifted the arguments for alternative explanations of the phenomena " (p. 245).

precarious, and in this connexion so misleading, as those to which attention is here directed. The survival of the soul is not resurrection.[1] An apparitional theory is not a theory of the Resurrection of Jesus as Apostolic Christianity understood it, but a substitute, which is in principle a negation, of the Apostolic affirmation.

It is speedily apparent, further, that apparitional theories of the Resurrection, quite as much as the visional, break on the character of the facts the theories are intended to explain. The empty tomb, once more, stands as an insuperable barrier in the way of all such theories. The testimony of the Apostles again stands on record, and cannot be spirited away. The witness of the Apostles was that they had actually seen and conversed with Jesus—not with an apparition or ghost of Jesus, but with the living Christ Himself. It is an acute criticism which the late Professor A. B. Bruce makes on Keim's " telegram " theory when he says : " It is open to the charge that it makes the faith of the disciples rest on a hallucination. Christ sends a series of telegrams from heaven to let His disciples know that all is well. But what does the telegram say in every case. Not merely, My spirit lives with God and cares for you ; but, My

---

[1] Prof. Lake says :. " What we mean by resurrection is not resuscitation of the material body, but the unbroken survival of personal life " (p. 265 ; cf. p. 275).

body is risen from the grave. . . . If the Resurrection be an unreality, if the body that was nailed to the tree never came forth from the tomb, why send messages that were certain to produce an opposite impression ? " [1]

After all, on such a theory supernaturalism is not escaped, and most will feel that Keim's spiritualistic hypothesis is a poor exchange for the Apostolic affirmation that Jesus actually burst the bands of death, and came forth living from the tomb, on the morning of the third day. Dr. Bruce says of it : " Truly this is a poor foundation to build Christendom upon, a bastard supernaturalism, as objectionable to unbelievers as the true supernaturalism of the Catholic creed, and having the additional drawback that it offers to faith asking for bread a stone." [2] It does not help much to plead that, if apparitions can be proved in the present day, the whole subject is brought within the domain of natural law. The reality of apparitions is never likely to be proved to the general satisfaction of mankind; but, if it were, they would certainly be regarded as facts belonging to a supernatural world, and not as mere phenomena of nature. The root of the whole difficulty, as Professor Lake frankly admits, is the naturalistic assumption that the reanimation of a dead body—

[1] *Apologetics*, p. 393.   [2] Ibid.

even of the body of the Son of God—could not take place.[1] Anything, he says, rather than that.[2], Hence the need of resorting to the fantastic theories just described, which yet, as seen, have an element of the supernatural inhering in them.

Visional and apparitional theories once parted with, there is only one remaining explanation, viz., *that the Resurrection really took place.* As Beyschlag truly says: " The *faith* of the disciples in the Resurrection of Jesus, which no one denies, cannot have originated, and cannot be explained otherwise than through the *fact* of the Resurrection, through the fact in its full, objective, supernatural sense, as hitherto understood." [3] So long as this is contested, the Resurrection remains a problem which rival attempts at explanation only leave in deeper darkness.

[1] *Ut supra*, pp. 264–5, 268–9.
[2] " Such a phenomena is in itself so improbable that any alternative is preferable to its assertion " (p. 267).
[3] *Leben Jesu*, i. p. 440.

NEO BABYLONIAN THEORIES—JEWISH AND APOCRYPHAL IDEAS

NEO-BABYLONIAN THEORIES—JEWISH AND APOCRYPHAL IDEAS

THE inadequacy of previous attempts to explain the Resurrection of Jesus out of natural grounds is convincingly shown by the rise of a new mythological school, which, discarding, or at least dispensing with, theories of vision and apparition, proposes to account for the " Resurrection-legend " —indeed for the whole New Testament Christology [1]—by the help of conceptions imported into Judaism from Babylonia and other parts of the Orient (Egyptian, Arabian, Persian, etc.). The rise of this school is connected particularly with the brilliant results of exploration in the East during the last half century, and with the consequent vast enlargement in our knowledge of peoples and religions of remote antiquity. The mythologies of these ancient religions—the study of comparative mythology generally—puts, it is thought, into the hands of scholars a golden key to open locks in Old

[1] Cf. Gunkel, *Zum religionsgeschichtlichen Verständniss des Neuen Testaments*, pp. 64, 89–95.

and New Testament religion which have hitherto remained closed to the most painstaking efforts of the learned.[1] The prestige which this new Babylonian school has already gained through its novelty and boldness of speculation entitles it to a consideration which, perhaps, if only its own merits were regarded, would hardly be accorded to it.

It is well to apprehend at the outset the position taken up by this revolutionary Babylonian school. It is the fact that myths of resurrection, though in vague, fluctuating form, to which the character of historical reality cannot for a moment be attached, are not infrequent in Oriental religions.[2] They are traceable in later even more than in earlier times, and specially are found in connection with the Mysteries. The analogies pressed into the service of their theories by scholars are often sufficiently shadowy,[3] but it is admitted that the myths used in the Mysteries and related festivals, whether Egyptian, Persian, Phrygian, Syrian, or Greek,

[1] Gunkel, p. 78: "Already in the Old Testament there are mysterious portions [he instances the "servant of Jehovah" in Isaiah] which hitherto have defied all attempts at interpretation," etc.

[2] For examples, see Cheyne, *Bible Problems*, pp. 119–22; Farnell, *The Evolution of Religion*, pp. 60–62; Frazer, *Golden Bough*, ii. pp. 115–168; Zimmern in Schrader's *Keilinschriften*, pp. 387 ff., 643.

[3] As when Zimmern connects this idea with the Babylonian god Marduk; or Cheyne (*ut supra*, p. 119) instances the myth of Osiris, "who after a violent death lived on in the person of his son Horus!"

had all a certain family likeness. They all turn, as Boissier remarks in his *La Religion Romaine*, on the death and resurrection of a god, and, in order still more to inflame the religious sensibility, in all the tales the god is loved by a goddess, who loses and refinds him, who mourns over his death, and ends by receiving him back to life. " In Egypt, it is Isis, who seeks Osiris, slain by a jealous brother ; in Phoenicia, it is Astarte or Venus who weeps for Adonis ; on the banks of the Euxine, it is Cybele, the great mother of the gods, who sees the beautiful Attis die in her arms." [1] Older than any of these, and, on the new theory, the parent of most of them, is the often-told Babylonian myth of Ishtar and Tammuz.[2] All, in truth, are nature-myths, telling the same story of the death of nature in winter, and its revival in spring, or of the conquest of light by darkness, and the return of brightness with the new sunrise [3] But in the Mysteries an allegorical significance was read into these myths, and they became the instruments of a moral symbolism, in which faint resemblances to Christian ideas can be discerned.

All this is old and tolerably familiar. But the

---

[1] Boissier, i. p. 408.

[2] See the story in full in Sayce's Hibbert Lectures, *The Religion of the Ancient Babylonians*, Lect. IV., " Tammuz and Ishtar."

[3] Cf. Gunkel, *ut supra*, p. 77 ; A. Jeremias, *Babylonisches im N.T.*, pp. 8 ff., 11, 19, etc.

Babylonian school goes much further. It is no longer parallels merely which are sought between the Gospel narratives and pagan myths, but an actual derivation is proclaimed. Ancient Babylonia had developed a comprehensive world-theory of which its mythology is the imaginative expression. These myths spread into all countries, receiving in each local modification; Israel, which came into contact with, and in Canaan deeply imbibed, this culture, could not escape being affected by it. Winckler, and in a more extreme form Jensen, find in Babylonian mythology the key not only to the so-called legends of the patriarchs, of Moses and Aaron, and of the Judges, but to the histories of Samuel, of Saul and David, of Elijah and Elisha. Now, by Gunkel, Cheyne, Jensen, and others, the theory is extended to the New Testament. Filtering down through Egypt, Canaan, Arabia, Phoenicia, Persia, there came, it is alleged, myths of virgin-births, of descents into Hades, of resurrections and ascensions; these, penetrating into Judaism, became attached to the figure of the expected Messiah—itself of old-world derivation—and gave rise to the idea that such and such traits would be realized in Him. Dr. Cheyne supposes that there was a written " pre-Christian sketch " of the Messiah, which embodied these features.[1] One form of the Jewish concep-

1 *Ut supra*, p. 128.

tion is seen in the picture of the woman clothed with the sun in Revelation xii. More definitely, the form which the conception assumed in Christian circles is seen in the legends of Christ's birth and infancy, in the incidents and miracles of His ministry, in the three days and nights of His burial in the tomb, and in the stories of His Resurrection and Ascension. It is the mythical theory of Strauss over again, with the substitution of Babylonian mythology for Old Testament prophecy as the foundation of an imaginary history of Jesus.

The shapes which this theory assumes in the hands of the writers who advocate it are naturally various. A few instances may be given.

Dr. Cheyne goes far enough in assuring us that "there are parts of the New Testament—in the Gospels, in the Epistles, and in the Apocalypse—which can only be accounted for by the newly-discovered fact of an Oriental syncretism which began early and continued late. And the leading factor in this is Babylonian." Among the beliefs the "mythic origin" of which is thus accounted for, is "the form of the belief in the Resurrection of Christ." [1] His "pre-Christian sketch" theory is alluded to below.

Gunkel's position is not dissimilar, and is wrought out in more detail. Judaism and Christianity, he

[1] *Bible Problems*, pp. 19, 117.

holds, are both examples of syncretism in religion.[1] Both are deeply penetrated by ideas diffused through the Orient, and derived chiefly from Babylonia. He states his thesis thus · " That in its origin and shaping (*Ausbildung*) the New Testament religion stood, in weighty, indeed essential points, under the decisive influence of foreign religions, and that this influence was transmitted to the men of the New Testament through Judaism." [2] He traces the penetrative influence of Oriental conceptions in Judaism, with special respect to the doctrine of the Resurrection ; [3] finds in it the origin of the Messianic idea, and of the Christology of St. Paul and St. John ; [4] and derives from it the Gospel narratives of the Infancy,[5] the Transfiguration,[6] the Resurrection from the dead on the third day,[7] the appearance to the disciples on the way to Emmaus,[8] the Ascension,[9] the origin of Sunday as a Christian festival,[10] etc.

A. Jeremias, from a believing standpoint, criticizes this position of Gunkel's, and the denial of

---

[1] *Ut supra*, pp. 34, 117. Judaism must be named " Eine synkretistische Religion." So, " Das Christentum ist eine synkretistische Religion."

[2] *Ut supra*, p. 1.   [3] Pp. 31–35.

[4] Pp. 24–5, 64, 89–95.   " The form of the Messiah belongs to this original mythological material " (p. 24).

[5] Pp. 65–70.

[6] P. 71 (likewise the Baptism and Temptation narratives, pp. 70–1).   [7] Pp. 76–83.   [8] P. 71.

[9] Pp. 71–2.   [10] Pp. 73–76.

the absoluteness of Christianity connected with it.[1] Sharing the same general view that " the Israelitish-Judaic background " of the New Testament writings " is no other than the Babylonian, or better, the old Oriental background," [2] he sees in the Babylonian mythology a pre-ordained providential preparation for the Gospel history and the Christian religion, the essential truths of which he accepts.[3] The resurrection of a god formed part of the universally-spread mythus.[4]

Everything hitherto attempted, however, in the application of this theory to the Biblical history is hopelessly left behind in the latest book which has appeared on the subject—Professor Jensen's *Das Gilgamesch-Epos in der Weltliteratur* of which, as yet, only the first volume has appeared. But this extends to 1,030 pages. It treats of the origins of the legends of the Old Testament patriarchs, prophets, and deliverers, and of the New Testament legend of Jesus, embracing all the incidents of His history—birth, life, miracles, death,

---

[1] *Bab. im N.T.*, p. 1.   [2] P. 3.

[3] Pp. 6, 46, 48, etc. The heathen myths are " Schattenbilder " (prefigurations, foreshadowings) of the Christian verities.

[4] Pp. 8–10. Jeremias has, however, little to say on the application to the Resurrection of Christ. He makes much more of the Virgin-birth (pp. 46 ff.). He says that no one who understands the circle of conceptions of the ancient Orient will doubt that Is. vii. 14, in the sense of the author, really means a " virgin " (p. 47).

and Resurrection. All, as the title suggests, are treated as transformations and elaborations of the old Babylonian epic of Gilgamesh and Eabani. We have Abraham-*Gilgamesh*, Jacob-*Gilgamesh*, Moses-*Gilgamesh*, Joshua-*Gilgamesh*, Samson-*Gilgamesh*, Samuel-*Gilgamesh*, Saul-*Gilgamesh*, David-*Gilgamesh*, Solomon-*Gilgamesh*, Elijah-*Gilgamesh*, Elisha-*Gilgamesh*, etc. With endless iteration the changes are rung on a few mythical conceptions; personages are blended, and attributes and incidents are transferred at will from one to another; the most far-fetched and impossible analogies are treated as demonstrations. The basis being laid in the Old Testament, the stories of John the Baptist and Jesus are then affiliated to the Gilgamesh myths through their supposed Old Testament parallels. For instance, the Resurrection of " Jesus-*Gilgamesh* " is supposed to be suggested by such incidents as the revival of the dead man cast into the grave of Elisha, on touching the bones of the prophet,[1] and the removal of the bones of Saul [2] and Samson [3] from their respective tombs ! [4] " Incredible, such trifling," one is disposed to exclaim. Not incredible, but the newest and truest " scientific " treatment of history, on the most approved " religionsgeschichtlichen "

---

[1] 2 Kings xiii. 21.   [2] 2 Sam. xxi. 12–14.
[3] Judges xvi. 31.
Gilgamesch-Epos, p. 923; cf. pp. 471, 697.

methods, thinks Jensen himself. The result, at least, in this author's learned pages, is the removal of the last particle of historicity from the life of Jesus in the Gospels. Such a person as Jesus of Nazareth " never existed "—" never lived." [1] " The Jesus-legend is an Israelitish *Gilgamesh*-legend," [2] attached to some person of whom we know absolutely nothing—neither time nor country. [3] " This Jesus has never walked the earth, has never died on earth, because He is actually *nought* but an Israelitish *Gilgamesh—nought* but a counterpart (*Seitenstück*) to Abraham, to Moses, and to innumerable other forms of the legend." [4]

It is needless to confront a reasoner like Jensen, confident in his multiplied proofs (?) that the Gospel history is throughout simply a Gilgamesh-legend, with the testimony of St. Paul. Everything that St. Paul has to tell of Jesus in his four accepted Epistles (Romans, 1 and 2 Corinthians, Galatians) belongs with the highest probability to the Gilgamesh-legend. [5] True, St. Paul tells how he abode fifteen days with St. Peter at Jerusalem, and then saw, and doubtless spoke with St. James, the Lord's brother ; and again how fourteen years later he met this same brother at Jerusalem. That is, he met the brother of this perfectly legendary character. [6] Jensen's reply is simple. Since the

[1] P. 1026. [2] P. 1024. [3] P. 1026.
[4] P. 1029. [5] P. 1027. [6] P. 1028.

Jesus of the Gospels and of the Epistles never existed, St. Paul could not have done what he describes. If these notices actually come from him, " the man either tells a falsehood, or he has been mystified in a wonderful way in Jerusalem." [1] It is a suspicious circumstance that St. Paul has to confirm his statement about seeing St. James with an oath.[2] It adds to the doubt that in 1 Corinthians xi., in its present form, this same St. Paul is found declaring that he received the quite mythical account of the institution of the Lord's Supper as a revelation of the Lord ! [3] " The ground here sinks beneath our feet." [4]

Jensen is an extremist, and his book may be regarded as the *reductio ad absurdum* of a theory which, before him, had been getting cut more and more away from the ground of historical fact. It is to that ground the endeavour must be made to bring it back. The Resurrection of Jesus, it has already been shown, is a fact which rests on historical evidence. What has the theory just described to say to this evidence ? It is a theory, obviously, which may be applied in different ways. It may be applied, e.g., to explain special *traits* in the narratives without denying the general facts of a death, a burial, and subsequent appearances of Jesus. It may be combined with a vision

---

[1] P. 1028. [2] Ibid.
[3] Ibid. [4] P. 1029.

theory, and used, as indeed in part it is, by A. Meyer [1] and Professor Lake, [2] to explain how the stories of these appearances came to take on their present form. Or, treating the whole account of the Resurrection as mythical, it may give itself no concern with the facts, and simply seek to account for the origin of the legend.

It is probably doing the theory no injustice to say that, in the hands of its chief exponents, it is the latter point of view which rules. There is no necessity for discussing the empty tomb, or the reality of Christ's appearances. Enough to show that the history, as we have it, is a deposit of mythological conceptions. Gunkel, e.g., excuses himself from discussion of the origin of faith in the Resurrection, [3] and confines himself to elucidating the form of the legend. Jensen, as just seen, regards the whole as a purely mythological growth. Cheyne has nearly as little to say on the historical basis. If this view be adopted, it cuts belief in the Resurrection away from the ground of history altogether, and it might be enough to reply to it —the history is *there*, and it is utterly impossible, by any legerdemain of the kind proposed, to get rid of it. You do not get rid of facts by simply proposing to give an artificial mythological ex-

---

[1] *Die Auferstehung Christi*, 184–5, 353–4.
[2] *Resur. of Jesus Christ*, pp. 260–3.
[3] Pp. 76–7.

planation of them. The Gospels, the Acts, and
the Epistles still stand, as containing the well-
attested accounts which the Church of Apostolic
days had to give of its own origin. These accounts
had not the remotest relation to Gilgamesh epics,
nature-myths of Egyptian, Greek, or Persian
Mysteries, or pagan speculations of any kind, but
were narratives of plain facts, known to the whole
Church, and attested by Apostles and others who
were themselves eye-witnesses of most of the things
which they related. It was the fact that on the
Friday the Lord was publicly crucified, and died ;
that He was buried in the tomb of Joseph of Arimathæa, in presence of many spectators ; that on
the morning of the third day—" the first day of
the week "—the tomb was visited by holy women,
who found it empty, and received the message
that Jesus had risen, as He said ; that on the same
day He appeared to individual disciples (Mary, St.
Peter, the disciples going to Emmaus), and, in the
evening, to the body of the disciples (the eleven) ;
that afterwards there were other appearances
which the Evangelists and St. Paul recount ; that,
after forty days, He was taken from them up to
heaven. The attempts to break down this history
have been studied in previous chapters, and proof
has been given that these attempts have failed.

Now, in lieu of the history, and as a new discovery, there is offered us this marvellous mytho-

logical construction, by which *all* history, and most previous theories of explanation as well, are swept into space. In dealing with it as a rival theory, not of the origin of belief in the Resurrection, for that it can hardly be said to touch, but of the Gospel story of the Resurrection, it must in frankness be declared of it that it labours under nearly every possible defect which a theory of the kind can have. This judgment it is necessary, but not difficult, to substantiate.

1. One thing which must strike the mind about the theory at once is the *baselessness* of its chief assumptions. Nothing need be said here of the general astral Babylonian hypothesis with which it starts, or of the assumed universal diffusion of this astral theory throughout the East. That must stand or fall on its own merits.[1] Nor need the traces of the influence of Oriental symbolism in Old Testament prophecy, or in Jewish and Christian Apocalyptic, be denied, if such really can be established. But what is to be said of the

[1] Winckler's theory on this subject is still the subject of much dispute among scholars (cf. Lake, *Resur. of Jesus Christ*, pp. 260–2). Prof. Lake says on its application to Scripture : " The difficulty is to decide how far this theory is based on fact, and how far it is merely guess-work " (p. 262). For a popular statement of Winckler's theory, see his *Die Babylonische Kultur in ihren Beziehungen zur unsrigen* (1902), and in criticism of Winckler and Jeremias, E. König, "*Altorientalische Weltanschauung*" *und Altes Testament*.

allegation, on the correctness of which the application to the New Testament depends, of a wholesale
absorption of Babylonian mythology by the Jewish
nation, and the crystallisation of this mythology
round the idea of the Messiah in Jewish popular
thought in pre-Christian times ? What proof worthy
of the name can be given of such an assumption ?
Dr. Cheyne's form of the theory, already referred
to, had best be stated in his own words. "The
four forms of Christian belief," he says, "which
we have been considering are the Virgin-birth of
Jesus Christ, His descent into the nether world,
His Resurrection, and His Ascension. On the
ground of facts supplied by archæology, it is plausible to hold that all these arose out of a pre-Christian sketch of the life, death, and exaltation of the
expected Messiah, itself ultimately derived from a
widely current mythic tradition respecting a solar
deity."[1] And earlier, "The Apostle Paul, when
he says (1 Cor. xv. 3, 4) that Christ died and that
He rose again 'according to the Scriptures,' in
reality points to a pre-Christian sketch of the life
of Christ, partly—as we have seen—derived from
widely-spread non-Jewish myths, and embodied
in Jewish writings."[2] With this drapery it is
assumed that the figure of Jesus of Nazareth was

[1] *Ut supra*, p. 128; cf. note xi., p. 252.
[2] P. 113. Gunkel may be compared, *ut supra*, pp. 68-9,
78-9.

clothed. But where is the faintest trace of evidence of such a pre-Christian Jewish sketch of the Messiah embracing Virgin-birth, Resurrection, and Ascension? It is nothing but an inferential conjecture from the Gospel narratives themselves, eked out by allusions to myths of deaths and resurrections of gods in other religions. These, as said above, are, in their origin, nature-myths. The Resurrection of Jesus was no nature-myth, but an event which happened three days after His Crucifixion, in an historical time, and in the case of an historical Personage. Parallels to *such* an event utterly fail.[1]

2. The baselessness of the foundation of the theory is only equalled by the *arbitrariness* of the methods by which a connexion with the Gospel, story is sought to be bolstered up. Specimens of Professor Jensen's reasonings have been given above, and no more need be said of them. But a like arbitrariness, if in less glaring form, infects

[1] Gunkel admits that " this belief in a dying and rising Christ was not present in *official* Judaism in the time of Jesus " ; but thinks it may have lurked " in certain private circles " (*ut supra*, p. 79). Cheyne, in his own note, can give no evidence at all of writings alluding to a resurrection (*ut supra*, p. 254).

Jesus and His Apostles found, indeed, a suffering and rising Christ in the O.T., but their point of view (on this see Hengstenberg, *Christology*, vol. iv., app. iv.) was not that of contemporary Judaism. The disciples themselves were " slow of heart " to believe the things that Jesus spoke to them (Luke xxiv. 25-6, 44-6).

the whole theory. In the Protean shapes assumed by Oriental mythology it is never difficult to pick out isolated traits which, by ingenious, if far-fetched combinations, can be made to present some resemblance to some feature or other in the Gospel story. Thus, as parallels to " the death of the world's Redeemer," we are told by Dr Cheyne : " That the death of the solar deity, Marduk, was spoken of, and his grave shown, in Babylonia, is an ascertained fact ; the death of Osiris and of other gods was an Egyptian belief, and, though a more distant parallel, one may here refer also to the empty grave of Zeus pointed out in Crete." [1] [Gunkel gives this last fact more correctly ; " In Crete is shown the grave of Zeus, naturally° an *empty* grave." [2]] Where facts fail, imagination is invoked to fill the gaps, this specially in the parts which concern the Resurrection. Thus, in Jeremias : " The ' grave of Bel ' (Herod. 1. 18), like the grave of Osiris, certainly stands in connexion (*zusammenhängt*) with the celebration of the death and resurrection of Marduk-Tammuz (Lehmann, i. p. 276), even *though we still possess no definite testimonies to a festival of the death and resurrection of Marduk-Tammuz* " [3] (italics ours). Gunkel thinks that the Jewish belief in the resur-erection compels us to " postulate " that " in the

Orient of that time belief in the resurrection must have ruled." [1]   Jensen has to face the fact, that the Gilgamesh epic has nothing about a resurrection.   But, he says, " that the Babyloniana Gilgamesh, who must die, in the oldest form of his legend (*Sage*) rose again from the dead, appears self-evident.   For he is a Sun-god, and sun-gods, like gods of light and warmth, who die, must also, among the Babylonians, rise again." [2]   The oldest form of the Elisha-*Gilgamesh* legend, he thinks probably included a translation to heaven, and, as an inference from this, a resurrection.[3] Similarly, the Resurrection of Jesus is a " logical postulate " from the fact of His exaltation, in accordance with a long series of parallel myths.[4]

A special application of the theory to the Gospel history connects itself with the Resurrection " on the third day," and the origin of the Sunday festival. It is very difficult, indeed, to find suitable illustrations connecting resurrection with " the third day "—indeed, none are to be found. We are driven back on Jonah's three days in the fish, which Dr. Cheyne says is not sufficient to justify St. Paul's expression ; [5] on the Apocalyptic " time and times and half a time," and three days and a half ; on a Mandæan story of a " little boy of

---

[1] *Ut supra*, p. 33.   [2] *Ut supra*, p. 925.
[3] Pp. 923-4.   [4] P. 924.
                [5] *Ut supra*, p. 254.

three years and one day "; on the Greek myth of
Apollo slaying the serpent Pytho on the fourth
day after his birth ; on the festival of the resurrection of the Phrygian Attis on the fourth day
after the lamentations over his death.[1] This is
actually supposed to be evidence. Gunkel makes
a strong point of the festival of Sunday. How
came the Resurrection of Jesus to be fixed down
to a Sunday ? How came this to be observed
as a weekly festival ? " All these difficulties are
relieved, so soon as we treat the matter from
the 'historical-religious' point of view "[2] The
" Lord's Day " was the day of the Sun-god ; in
Babylonian reckoning the first day of the week.
Easter Sunday was the day of the sun's emergence
from the night of winter.[3] Can it be held, then,
as accidental that this was the day on which Jesus
arose ?[4] It is really an ancient Oriental festival
which is here being taken over by the primitive
Christian community, as later the Church took
over December 25 as Christmas Day.[5] It fails to
be observed in this ingenious construction—wholly
in the air, as if there was no such thing as history
in the matter—that there is not a single word in

---

[1] Pp. 110–13 ; cf. Gunkel, *ut supra*, pp. 79–82 ; Lake,
p. 263.

[2] Gunkel, p. 74.

[3] Pp. 74, 79. Thus also Loisy, *Les Évangiles Synoptiques*, ii. p. 721.

[4] P. 79.   [5] Pp. 74–5, 79.

the Gospels or in the New Testament connecting
" the first day of the week "—reckoned in purely
Jewish fashion by the " Sabbath "—with the day
of the sun, or any use or suggestion of the name
" Sunday." The " primitive community " had
other and far plainer reasons for remembrance
of the " Lord's Day " (Jesus alone was their " Lord,"
and no sun-god), viz., in the fact that on the Friday
of the Passover week He was crucified and en-
tombed, and on the dawn of the first day of the
week thereafter actually came forth, as He had
predicted, victorious over the power of death, and
appeared to His disciples.

This theory, in brief, destitute of adequate foundation, laden with incredibilities, and disdainful
of the world of realities, has no claim whatever
to supersede the plain, simply-told, historically
well-attested narratives of the four Gospels as to
the grounds of the Church's belief from the beginning in the Resurrection of the Lord from the
dead. As has frequently been said in these pages
—*the Church knew its own origin*, and could be
under no vital mistake as to the great facts on
which its belief in Christ as its Crucified and Risen
Lord rested. It is difficult to imagine what kind
of persons the Apostles and Evangelists in some
of these theories are taken for—children or fools?
They were really neither, and the work they did,
and the literature they have left, prove it. Who

that has ever felt on his spirit the power of the impression of the picture and teaching of Jesus in the Gospels could dream of accounting for it by a bundle of Babylonian myths? Who that has ever experienced the power of His Resurrection life could fancy the source of it an unreality?

It may be appropriate at this point to say a few words on the state of *Jewish belief* on the subject of resurrection That the Jews in the time of Jesus were familiar with the idea of a resurrection of the dead (the Sadducees alone denying it [1]) is put beyond question by the Gospels,[2] though there is no evidence, despite assertions to the contrary,[3] that they connected death and resurrection with the idea of the Messiah. The particular ideas entertained by the Jews of the resurrection-body,[4] while of interest in themselves, have therefore only a slight bearing on the origin of belief in the Resurrection of Jesus from His tomb on the third day. That was an event *sui generis*, outside the anticipations of the disciples, notwithstanding the repeated intimations which Jesus Himself had given them regarding it,[5] and

[1] Matt. xxii. 23, etc.; cf. Acts xxiii. 6–8.
[2] As above; cf. John v. 28, 29; xi. 24; Matt. xiv. 2; and the instances of resurrection in the Gospels (Jairus's daughter, son of widow of Nain, Lazarus).
[3] Gunkel and Cheyne give no proof, and none is to be had
[4] On these, cf. Lake, *ut supra*, pp. 23–7, with references.
[5] As already seen, these were persistently misunder-

only forced upon their faith by indubitable evidence of the actual occurrence of the marvel. There is no reason to suppose that the idea of the resurrection of the body was a form subsequently imposed on a belief in the Lord's continued life [1] originally gained in some other way. The Resurrection of Jesus never meant anything else in the primitive community than His Resurrection in the body.

Of greater importance is the question raised by Gunkel in his discussion as to *whence* the Jews derived their idea of the resurrection. It is to be granted that Gunkel has a much profounder view of what he calls " the immeasurable significance " of this doctrine of the resurrection for the New Testament [2] than most other writers who deal with the topic. He claims that " this doctrine of the resurrection from the dead is one of the greatest things found anywhere in the history of religion," [3] and devotes space to drawing out its weighty implications. Just, however, on account of " this incomparable significance " of the doctrine, he holds that it cannot be derived from within Judaism itself, but must take its origin from a ruling belief in the Orient of the later time. [4] The existence of such a belief is a " postulate " from its presence

---

stood by the disciples. The critics mostly deny that they were given.

[1] Thus Harnack and others.

[2] *Ut supra*, p. 31.　　　[3] P. 32.　　　[4] P. 33.

in Judaism, and is thought to be supported by Oriental, especially by Egyptian and Persian, parallels.[1] He discounts the evidence of the belief in the Old Testament furnished by passages in the Psalms, the prophets, and in Job. The doctrine, in short, " is not, as was formerly commonly maintained, and sometimes still is maintained, a genuine product of Judaism, but has come into Judaism from without." [2] If this be so, it may be argued that it is really a pagan intrusion into Christianity, and ought not to be retained.

The " immeasurable significance " of the belief in resurrection among the Jews may be admitted, but Gunkel's inferences to the foreign origin of the belief can only be contested. For—

1. The *link fails* to connect this belief with any foreign religions. Gunkel seems hardly aware of the paradox of his theory of a world filled with belief in the resurrection, while yet the Jews, till a late period, are supposed to have had no knowledge of it. But the theory itself is without foundation. There is no evidence of any such *general* belief in a resurrection of the dead in ancient religions. No evidence of such general belief can be adduced from ancient Babylonia. Merodach may be hailed in a stray verse as " the merciful one, who raises the dead to life," and Ishtar may rescue Tammuz from Hades. But this falls far

---

[1] P. 33.   [2] P. 31.

short of the proof required. Belief in the re-animation of the body may underlie the Egyptian practice of embalming, though this is disputed, but the developed Osiris-myth is comparatively late, and without provable influence on Judaism.[1] The alleged Persian or Zoroastrian influence is equally problematical. It is very questionable how far this doctrine is found in the old Persian religion at all.[2] The references to it are certainly few and ambiguous,[3] and totally inadequate to explain the remarkable prominence which the doctrine assumed among the Jews.

2. The *adequate grounds* for the development of this doctrine are found in the Old Testament itself. It may be held, and has been argued for by the present writer,[4] that, so far as a hope of immortality (beyond the shadowy and cheerless lot of Sheol) appears in the Old Testament, it is

[1] On Merodach, Osiris and Resurrection, cf. Sayce, *Religions of Ancient Egypt and Babylonia*, pp. 24, 153 ff., 165, 168, 288, 329, etc.

[2] Schultz remarks : " This point [of influence] will be the more difficult to decide, the more uncertain it becomes how far this doctrine, the principal witness to which is the Bundehesh [a late work], was really Old Persian " (*O.T. Theol.* ii. p. 392).

[3] This can be tested by consulting the translation to the Zend-Avesta in *The Sacred Books of the East*. The indexes to the three volumes give only one reference to the subject, and that to an undated " Miscellaneous Fragment " at the end.

[4] In *The Christian View of God and the World :* Appendix to Lect. V., " The Old Testament Doctrine of Immortality."

always in the form of deliverance from Sheol, and renewed life in the body. The state of death is neither a natural nor normal state for man, whose original destiny was immortality in the completeness of his personal life in a body; and the same faith which enabled the believer to trust in God for deliverance from all ills of life, enabled him also, in its higher exercises, to trust Him for deliverance from death itself. This seems the true key to those passages in the Psalms and in Job which by nearly all but the new school of interpreters have been regarded as breathing the hope of immortality with God.[1] In the prophets, from Hosea down, the idea of a resurrection of the nation, including, may we not say, at least in such passages as Hosea vi. 2; xiii. 14, and Isaiah xxv. 6–8; xxvi. 19, the individuals in it, is a familiar one. A text like Daniel xii. 2 only draws out the individual implication of this doctrine with more distinctness. In later books, as 2 Maccabees, the Book of Enoch, Ezra iv., the doctrine is treated as established (sometimes resurrection of the godly, sometimes of righteous and wicked).

[1] E.g., Pss. xvi. 8–11; xvii. 15; xlix. 14, 15; lxxiii. 24; Job xiv. 13–15 (R.V.); xix. 25–27. In his *Origin of the Psalter* Dr. Cheyne accepts the resurrection reference of several of these passages, seeing in them a proof of Zoroastrian influence (pp. 382, 406, 407, 431, etc.). This, however, as he himself acknowledges, is where leading scholars fail to support him (pp. 425, 451). Cf. Pusey, Daniel, pp. 512–17.

Little has been said in these discussions of the New Testament *Apocryphal* books,[1] the statements of which it has become customary to draw into comparison with the accepted Gospels. Only a few remarks need be made on them now. They have been kept apart because, in origin, character, and authority, they stand on a completely different footing from the canonical Gospels, and because there is not the least reason to believe that they preserve a single authentic tradition beyond those which the four Gospels contain. This has long been acknowledged with regard to the stories of the Infancy, the puerilities of which put them outside the range of serious consideration by any intelligent mind. No more reason exists for paying heed to the fabulous embellishments of the narratives of the Resurrection. A romance like *The Gospel of Nicodemus* (fifth cent.), whether based on a second century *Acts of Pilate* or not, receives attention from no one. It is simply a travesty and tricking out with extravagances of the material furnished by St. Matthew and the other Evangelists. More respect is paid to the recently-discovered fragment of *The Gospel of Peter*,[2] which begins in the middle of Christ's trial, and breaks

---

[1] A collection of some of the chief of these, edited and annotated by the present writer, may be seen in *The New Testament Apocryphal Writings*, in the " Temple Bible " series (Dent).

[2] A Gnostic Gospel of the 2nd century.

off in the middle of a sentence, with Peter and
Andrew returning to their fishermen's toils, after
the feast of unleavened bread is ended. Here,
it is thought, is a distinct tradition, preserving
the memory of that flight into Galilee which the
canonical Gospels ignore. Yet at every point
this Gospel shows itself dependent on St. Matthew
and the rest, while freely manipulating and embellishing the tradition which they contain. A single
specimen is enough to show the degree of credit
to be attached to it. From St. Matthew is borrowed the story of the watch at the tomb, with
adornments, the centurion, e.g., being named
Petronius. The day of the Resurrection is called
" the Lord's Day." Then, we read, as that• day
dawned, " While the soldiers kept watch two and
two at their post, a mighty voice sounded in the
heaven ; and they saw the heavens opened, and
two men descending from thence in great glory,
and approaching the sepulchre. But that stone
which had been placed at the door of the sepulchre
rolled back of itself, and moved aside, and the
tomb opened, and both the young men went in.
When, therefore, those soldiers beheld this, they
awakened the centurion and the elders—for they
also were there to watch—and while they were
telling what they had seen, they behold coming
forth from the tomb three men, and the two sup-
porting the one, and a cross following them. And

the heads of the two reached indeed unto heaven, but the head of the one who was led by them reached far above the heavens. And they heard a voice from heaven that said: Hast thou preached unto those that sleep? And the answer was heard from the Cross: Yes. . . . And while they were yet pondering the matter, the heavens open again, and a man descends and goes into the sepulchre." [1] This may be placed alongside of the narrative in the Gospel without comment.

[1] If it is argued that this is a simple expansion of St. Matthew's story of the watch, as the latter is an addition to St. Mark's, it may be observed that St. Matthew's story is an expansion or embellishment of nothing, but a distinct, independent narrative; while the story in *The Gospel of Peter* has evidently no basis but St. Matthew's account, which it decorates from pure fancy.

DOCTRINAL BEARINGS OF THE RESURRECTION

X

DOCTRINAL BEARINGS OF THE RESUR-
RECTION

It will probably be evident from the preceding discussion that a movement is at present in process which aims at nothing less than the dissolution of Christianity, as that has hitherto been understood. It is not simply the details of the recorded life of Jesus that are questioned, but the whole conception of Christ's supernatural Person and work, as set forth in the Gospels and Epistles, which is challenged. If the Virgin Birth is rejected at one end of the history, and the bodily Resurrection at the other, not less are the miracles and supernatural claims that lie between. With this goes naturally on the part of many a hesitancy in admitting even Christ's moral perfection.[1] A sinless Personality would be a miracle in time, and miracles are excluded by the first principles of the new philosophy.

[1] This tendency is seen in various recent pronouncements. E.g., Mr. G. L. Dickinson, in the *Hibbert Journal* for April, 1908, asks : "How many men are really aware of any such personal relation to Jesus as the Christian religion presupposes ? How many, if they told the honest truth, really hold Him to be even the ideal man ? " (p. 522).

Bolder spirits, taking, as they conceive, a wider outlook on the field of religion, and on the evolutionary advance of the race, would cut loose the progress of humanity from Christianity altogether.[1] It is an illusion to imagine that a tendency of this kind can be effectively met by any half-way, compromising attitude to the great supernatural facts on which Christianity rests. It is only to be met by the firm reassertion of the whole truth regarding the Christ of the New Testament Gospel—a Christ supernatural in origin, nature, works, claims, mission, and destiny; the divine Son, incarnate for the salvation of the world, pure from sin, crucified and risen, ever-living to carry on to its consummation the work of the Kingdom He founded while on earth. None need really fear that the ground is about to be swept from beneath his feet with respect to this divine foundation by any skill of sceptics or revolutionary discoveries in knowledge. One notices in how strange ways the wheel of criticism itself comes round often to the affirmation of things it once denied. To take only one point: how often has the contrast between the Jesus of the Synoptics and the Pauline and Johannine Christ been emphasized? The contrast is, of course, still maintained, yet with the growing admission that the difference is at most one of *degree*, that the Jesus

---

[1] The same writer rejects Christianity, and advocates a return to " mythology " (p. 509).

of the Synoptics is as truly a supernatural being as
the Jesus of St. John. Bousset, e.g., states this
frankly : " Already," he says, " the oldest Gospel
is written from the standpoint of faith ; already for
Mark is Jesus not only the Messiah of the Jewish
people, but the miraculous eternal Son of God, whose
glory shone in this world.   And it has been rightly
emphasized, that in this respect, our first three
Gospels are distinguished from the fourth only in
degree. . . . For the faith of the community,
which the oldest Evangelist already shares, Jesus is
the miraculous Son of God, in whom men believe,
whom men put wholly on the side of God." [1]

In the history of such a Christ as the Gospels
depict the Resurrection from the dead has its natural
and necessary place. To the first preachers of
Christianity an indissoluble connexion subsisted
between the Resurrection of Jesus and the Gospel
they proclaimed. Remove that foundation, and
in St. Paul's judgment, their message was gone.
" If Christ hath not been raised," he says, " then is

[1] *Was wissen wir von Jesus ?* pp. 54, 57. To explain
these traits some scholars feel it necessary to postulate
a revision of St. Mark's Gospel from a Johannine standpoint. Thus J. Weiss, in the *Dict. of Christ and the Gospels,*
ii. p. 324 : " For our own part we have been able to collect
a mass of evidence in support of the theory that the text
of Mark has been very thoroughly revised from the Johannine standpoint, that a host of Johannine characteristics
were inserted into it at some period subsequent to its use
by Matthew and Mark." There is no real proof of such
revision.

our preaching vain, your faith also is vain.   If
Christ hath not been raised, your faith is vain ; ye
are yet in your sins." [1] To " modern " thought,
on the other hand, the Resurrection of Jesus, in
any other sense, at least, than that of spiritual survival, has no essential importance for Christianity.
The belief in a bodily Resurrection is rather an
excrescence on Christianity, that can be dropped
without affecting it in any vital way.   Is this really
so ?   It may aid faith if it can be shown that, so
far from being a non-essential of Christianity, the
Resurrection of Jesus is, as the Apostles believed,
in the strictest sense, a *constitutive* part of the
Christian Gospel.

   1. In the older mode of treatment of the Resurrection, peculiar stress was laid upon its *evidential*
value.   It was the culminating proof of Christ's
claim to be " a Teacher come from God," [2] or, from
a higher point of view, the crowning demonstration
of His divine Sonship and Messiahship.   It was also
the supreme attestation of the fact of immortality.
The angle of vision is now considerably changed, and
it has rightly become more customary to view the
Resurrection in the light of Christ's claims and manifested glory as the Son of God, than to regard the
latter as deriving credibility from the former.   But
care must be taken that the element of truth in the
older view is likewise conserved.

[1] I Cor. xv. 14.   [2] John iii. 2,

(1) With respect to the *divine Sonship*. It is doubtless the case that faith in the Resurrection is connected with, and in part depends on, the degree of faith in Jesus Himself. It is the belief that Jesus is such an One as the Gospels represent Him to be—"holy, guileless, undefiled, separated from sinners,"[1] divinely great in the prerogatives He claims as Son of God and Saviour of the world, yet in His submission to rejection and death at the hands of sinful men the perfect example of suffering obedience—which above all sustains the conviction that He, the Prince and Lord of life, cannot have succumbed to the power of death, and prepares the mind to receive the evidence that He actually *did* rise, as the Gospels declare.

This connexion of faith in the Resurrection with faith in Jesus, however, it must now be remarked, in no way deprives the Resurrection of Jesus of the apologetic or evidential value which justly belongs to it as a fact of the first moment, amply attested on its own account, in its bearings on the Lord's Person and claims. The attempt to set faith and historical evidence in opposition to each other, witnessed specially in the Ritschlian school, must to the general Christian intelligence, always fail. Since, as is above remarked, it is implied in Christ's whole claim that He, the Holy One, should not be holden of death,[2] not merely that He has a spiritual

[1] Heb. vii. 26.
[2] Acts ii. 24. This is further illustrated below.

life with God—faith would be involved in insoluble contradictions if it could be shown that Christ has not risen, or, what comes to the same thing, that there is no historical evidence that He has risen. It may be, and is, involved in faith that He should rise from the dead, but this faith would not of itself be a sufficient ground for asserting that He had risen, if all historical evidence for the statement were wanting. Faith cherishes the just expectation that, if Christ has risen, there will be historical evidence for the fact ; and were such evidence not forthcoming, it would be driven back upon itself in questioning whether its confidence was not self-delusion.

In harmony with this view is the place which the Resurrection of Jesus holds in Scripture, and the stress there laid upon its historical attestation. "Declared," the Apostle says, "to be the Son of God with power, according to the Spirit of holiness, by the Resurrection of the dead." [1] It is undeniable that, if historically real, the Resurrection of Jesus is a confirmation of His entire claim. No mind can believe in that transcendent fact, and in the exaltation that followed it, and continue to apply to Christ a mere humanitarian standard. The older Socinians attempted this, but the logic of the case proved too strong for them. Both assertions hold good: Christ's Personality and claims demand a Resurrection, and, conversely, the Resurrection is a retro-

[1] Rom. i. 4.

spective attestation that Jesus was indeed the exalted and divinely-sent Person He claimed to be.

(2) Not very dissimilar is the position to be taken as to the evidential value of the Resurrection with regard to *immortality*. The relation here is, indeed, more vital than at first appears. The Christian hope, it will immediately be seen, is not merely that of an " immortality of the soul," nor is " eternal life " simply the indefinite prolongation of existence in a future state of being. Keeping, however, at present to the general question of the possibility and reality of a life beyond the grave, it is to be asked what bearing the Resurrection of Jesus has as evidence on this. None whatever, a writer like Professor Lake will reply, for the physical Resurrection is an incredibility, and can prove nothing. Apparitional manifestations are possible, but even these can only be admitted if, first of all, proof is given of the survival of the soul by the help of such phenomena as the Society of Psychical Research furnishes.[1] Others base on the natural grounds for belief in a future life supplied by the constitution of the human soul, eked out, in the case of recent able writers, by appeal to the same class of psychical phenomena.[2] On a more

[1] *Res. of Jesus Christ*, pp. 245, 272–3.
[2] Cf. the interesting paper on Immortality by Sir Oliver Lodge in the *Hibbert Journal* for April, 1908. The persistence of the soul (which damage or destruction of the brain is held not to disprove) is argued from the " priority in essence of the spiritual to the material " and from such

spiritual plane, Herrmann and Harnack would argue that immortality is given as a " thought of faith " in the direct contemplation of Christ's life in God· A soul of such purity, elevation, and devotion to the Father as was Christ's cannot be thought of as extinguished in death.[1]

It seems evident that, if man is really a being destined for life hereafter, indications of this vast destiny cannot be absent from the make and constitution of his nature.   Capacities will reveal themselves in him proportionate to the immortality that awaits him.   It is not denied, therefore—at least here—that there are grounds in man's nature abundantly warranting a reasonable faith in a life beyond death, and awakening the craving for more light regarding that future state of being.   History and literature, however, are witnesses how little these " natural intimations of immortality " can of themselves do to sustain an assured confidence in a future conscious existence, or to give comfort and hope at the thought of entrance into it.   Browning may be styled a poet of immortality, but a long distance is traversed between the early optimism of a *Pauline*,[2] and the soul-racking doubts of a *La Saisiaz*, when

facts as telepathy (pp. 570 ff.), præter-normal psychology (pp. 572 ff.), automatism (pp. 574 ff.), subliminal faculty (pp. 547 ff.), genius (pp. 580 ff.), mental pathology (pp. 582 ff.).

[1] Cf. Herrmann, *Communion with God* (E. T.), pp. 221–2.
[2] Cf. Browning, *Works*, i. pp. 27, 29.

the question has to be faced and answered in the light of reason, " Does the soul survive the body ? Is there God's self, no or yes ? "[1]

The spiritual faith that roots itself in Christ's unbroken communion with the Father has, indeed, an irrefragable basis. But is it adequate, if it does not advance to its own natural completion in belief in the Resurrection ? For Christ's earthly history does not end as an optimistic faith would expect. Rather, it closes in seeming defeat and disaster. The forces of evil—the powers of dissolution that devour on every side—seem to have prevailed over Him also. Is this the last word ? If so, how shall faith support itself ?   " We hoped that it was He which should redeem Israel."[2] Is not the darkness deeper than before when even He seems to go down in the struggle ?

Will it be doubted that, as for the first disciples, so for myriads since, the Resurrection has dispelled these doubts, and given them an assurance which nothing can overthrow that death is conquered,[3] and that, because Jesus lives, they shall live also ?[4] Jesus, who came from God and went to God, has shed a flood of light into that unseen world which has vanquished its terrors, and made it the bright home of every spiritual and eternal hope. It is open to any one to reject this consolation, grounded

---

[1] *Works*, xiv. p. 168.   [2] Luke xxiv. 21.
[3] 1 Cor. xv. 54-7.   [4] John xiv. 19.

in sure historical fact, or to prefer to it the star-light—if even such it can be named—of dubious psychical phenomena. But will it be denied that for those who, on what they judge the best of grounds, *believe* the Resurrection, there is opened up a " sure and certain hope " of immortality which nothing else in time can give ?

2. The Resurrection is an evidential fact, and its importance in this relation is not to be minimized. But this, as a little consideration may show, after all, only touches the exterior of the subject. The core of the matter is not reached till it is perceived that the Resurrection of Jesus is not simply an external seal or evidential appendage to the Christian Gospel, but enters as a *constitutive element* into the very essence of that Gospel. Its denial or removal would be the mutilation of the Christian doctrine of Redemption, of which it is an integral part. An opposite view is that of Herrmann, who lays the whole stress on the impression produced by Christ's earthly life. Such a view has no means of incorporating the Resurrection into itself as a constitutive part of its Christianity. The Resurrection remains at most a deduction of faith without inner relation to salvation ? It is apt to be felt, therefore, to be a superfluous appendage. In a full Scriptural presentation it is not so. It might almost be said to be a test of the adequacy of the view of Christ and His work taken by any school, whether

it is able to take in the Resurrection of Christ as
a constitutive part of it.

In New Testament Scripture, it will not be
disputed that these two things are always taken
together—the Death and the Resurrection of Christ
—the one as essentially connected with, and completed in, the other. " It is Christ Jesus that died,"
says St. Paul, " yea, rather, that was raised from
the dead." [1] " Who was delivered up for our
trespasses, and was raised for our justification." [2]
" Who through Him," says St. Peter, " are believers
in God, which raised Him from the dead, and gave
Him glory ; so that your faith and hope might be
in God." [3] " The God of peace, who brought
again from the dead the great shepherd of the sheep,
with the blood of the everlasting covenant," [4]
we read in Hebrews. " I am the Living One ; and
I was dead, and behold, I am alive for evermore," [5]
says the Lord in the Apocalypse.

What is the nature of this connexion ? The
answer to this question turns on the manner in
which the death of Christ itself is conceived, and
on this point the teaching of the New Testament is
again sufficiently explicit. The Cross is the decisive
meeting-place between man's sin and God's grace.
It is the point of reconciliation between man and

---

[1] Rom. viii. 34.   [2] Rom. iv. 25.
[3] 1 Pet. i. 21 ; cf. iii. 18–22.   [4] Heb. xiii. 20.
[5] Rev. i. 18.

God. *There* was accomplished—at least consummated—the great work of Atonement for human sin ! Christ, as the Epistle to the Hebrews declares, " put away sin by the sacrifice of Himself." [1]

It seems superfluous to quote passages in illustration of a truth of which the Apostolic writings are literally full. Jesus Himself laid stress on His death as a means of salvation to the world,[2] and, theories apart, every principal writer in the New Testament reiterates the idea in every form of expression which the vocabulary of Redemption can yield. But, if this is the true light in which the death of Jesus through and for the sin of man is to be conceived, how does the Resurrection of Jesus stand related to it ? Is it an accident ? Or is there not connexion of the most vital kind ? Manifestly there is, and that in various respects.[3]

(1) The connexion at the outset is an essential one with *Christ's own work* as Redeemer. One need only follow here the familiar lines of Apostolic teaching, in which the Resurrection is represented under such aspects as the following :—

i. As the natural and necessary *completion* of the work of Redemption itself. Accepting the

---

[1] Heb. ix. 26.

[2] Matt. xx. 28 ; xxvi. 26–28 ; John iii. 14–16, etc.

[3] For an interesting treatment of this whole subject, cf. Milligan, *The Resurrection of Our Lord*, Lects. IV., V. and VI.

above interpretation of Christ's death, it seems evident that, if Christ died for men—in Atonement for their sins—it could not be that He should remain permanently in the state of death. That, had it been possible, would have been the frustration of the very end of His dying, for if He remained Himself a prey to death, how could He redeem others? Jesus Himself seldom spoke of His death without coupling it with the prediction of His Resurrection.[1] St. Peter in Acts assumes it as self-evident that it was not possible that death should hold Him.[2] St. Paul constantly speaks of the Resurrection as the necessary sequel of the Crucifixion, and directly connects it with justification.[3] The further point —that a complete Redemption of man includes the redemption of the body—is dwelt upon below.

ii. As *the Father's seal* on Christ's completed work, and public declaration of its *acceptance*. Had Christ remained a prey to death, where would have been the knowledge, the certainty, the assurance that full Atonement had indeed been made, that the Father had accepted that holy work on behalf of our sinful race, that the foundation of perfect reconciliation between God and man had indeed been laid? With the Resurrection a public demonstration was given, not only, as before, of Christ's divine Sonship and Messiahship, but of the

---

[1] Matt. xvi. 21 ; xvii. 23 ; xx. 19 ; John x. 17, 18, etc.
[2] Acts ii. 24.   [3] Rom. iv. 25.

Father's perfect satisfaction with, and full acceptance of the whole work of Christ as man's Saviour,
but peculiarly His work as Atoner for sin, expressed
in such words as " Christ died for the ungodly," [1]
" Who His own self bare our sins in His body upon
the tree." [2]   It is this which leads St. Paul to connect the assurance of justification—of forgiveness,
of freedom from all condemnation—with faith in
the Resurrection.[3] The ground of acceptance was
the obedience unto death upon the Cross, but it was
the Resurrection which gave the joyful confidence
that the work had accomplished its result.

iii. As the entrance of Christ on a new life as the
risen and exalted Head of His Church and *universal
Lord.* The Resurrection of Jesus is everywhere
viewed as the commencement of His Exaltation.
Resurrection, Ascension, Exaltation to the throne
of universal dominion go together as parts of the
same transaction.[4]   St. Paul, in Acts, connects the
Resurrection with the words of the second Psalm,
" Thou art My Son, this day have I begotten Thee." [5]
But the Resurrection, as the New Testament writers

---

[1] Rom. v. 6.   [2] 1 Pet. ii. 24.
[3] Rom. iv. 24, 25 ; viii. 35 ; x. 9.
[4] Cf. e.g. Rom. viii. 34 ; Eph. i. 20–22 ; iii. 9, 10 ; Heb.
iv. 14 ; x. 12 ; 1 Pet. iii. 21–2.   On this ground Harnack
argues against the separation of the Ascension from the
Resurrection in the Creed (*Das. Apost. Glaubensbekenntniss*
p. 25).   But cf. Swete, *The Apostles' Creed*, pp. 64 ff.).
[5] Acts xiii. 33.

likewise testify, was a change of *state*—from the
temporal to the eternal, from humiliation to glory,
above all, from a condition which had to do with
sin, and the taking away of sin, to one which is
" apart from sin " (χωρὶς ἁμαρτίας),[1] and is marked
by the plenitude of spiritual power. This is a prevailing view in St. Paul and in the Epistle to the
Hebrews. " The death that He died," says the
former, " He died unto sin once : but the life that
He liveth, He liveth unto God."[2] " The last Adam
became a life-giving Spirit."[3] " When He had
made purification of sins," says the latter, He " sat
down on the right hand of the Majesty on high."[4]
" Having been made perfect, He became unto all
them that obey Him the author of eternal salvation."[5] " He, when He had offered one sacrifice
for sins for ever, sat down on the right hand of
God, from henceforth expecting till His enemies
be made the footstool of His feet."[6] A priest
" after the power of an endless life."[7] With
His exaltation is connected the gift of the Spirit.
" Being therefore," said St. Peter, " by the
right hand of God exalted, and having received
of the Father the promise of the Holy Ghost, He
hath poured forth this, which ye see and hear."[8]

[1] Heb. ix. 28.
[2] Rom. vi. 10.   [3] 1 Cor. xv. 45.   [4] Heb. i. 3.
[5] Heb. v. 9.   [6] Heb. x. 12, 13.   [7] Heb. vii. 16.
[8] Acts ii. 33.   Cf. Christ's own promises, John xiv. 16,
26 ; xv. 26 ; xvi. 7.

On this view of Jesus as having died to sin, and risen
in power to a new life with God, and having become
the principle of spiritual quickening to His people,
is based what is sometimes spoken of as St. Paul's
" mystical " doctrine of the union of believers with
Christ. Through faith, and symbolically in baptism, the Christian dies with Christ to sin—is thence-
forth done with it as something put away and
belonging to the past—and rises with Him in spiritual power to newness of life.[1]   Christ lives in him
by His Spirit.[2]   He is risen with Christ, and shares
a life the spring of which is hid with Christ in God.[3]
Is it possible to review such testimonies without
realizing how tremendous is the significance attached
in Apostolic Christianity to this fact of the Resurrection ?

(2) A further aspect of the doctrinal significance
of the resurrection [is opened when it is observed
that the Resurrection is not simply the completion of Christ's redemptive work, but, in one important particular, itself sheds light on the *nature*
of that redemption.   It does so inasmuch as it
gives its due place to the *body* of man in the constitution of his total personality.   Man is a com
pound being.   The body as well as the soul enters
into the complete conception of his nature.   The
redemption of the whole man, therefore, includes,

---

[1] Rom. vi. 3–11.
[2] Rom. viii. 9–11 ; Gal. i. 20.   [3] Col. iii. 1–3.

as St. Paul phrases it, " the adoption, to wit, the redemption of the body."[1] From this point of view it may be said that the Resurrection was essential in that the redemption of man meant the redemption of his whole personality, body and soul together. A mere *spiritual* survival of Christ— an " immortality of the soul " only—would not have been sufficient. This is a consideration which has its roots deep in the Scripture doctrine of man, and has important bearings on the subject of resurrection.

It was remarked earlier that the Christian doctrine of immortality is not simply that of a survival of death, and future state of existence of the *soul*. The spiritual part of man is indeed that in which his God-like qualities reveal themselves—in which he bears the stamp of the divine image. It is the seat of his rational, moral, self-conscious, personal life. It is that which proves him to be more than a being of nature—a transient bubble on the heaving sea of physical change, and proclaims his affinity with the Eternal. Idealism emphasizes this side of man's nature, and almost forgets that there is another equally real. For, if man is a spiritual existence, he appears not less as the crown of nature's development, and as bound by a thousand ties through a finely-adjusted bodily organisation to the physical and animal world from which he has

---

[1] Rom. viii. 23.

emerged. Naturalism, in turn, lays stress on the latter side of his being, and is tempted to ignore the former. It explains man as a product of physical forces, and treats immortality as a chimera. A true view of man's nature will embrace both sides. It will acknowledge the spiritual dignity of man, but will recognize that he is not, and was never intended to be, pure spirit ; that he is likewise a denizen of the natural world endowed with corporeity, residing in, and acting through a body which is as truly a part of *himself* as life or soul itself is. He is, in short, the preordained link between two worlds—the natural and the spiritual ; and has relation in his personality to both. He is not spirit simply, but incorporated spirit.   •

If this is a true view to take of man's nature—and it is held here to be the Biblical view,[1] it directly affects the ideas to be formed of death and immortality. Death, in the case of such a being, however it may be with the animal, can never be a merely natural event. Body and soul—integral elements in man's personality—cannot be sundered without mutilation and loss to the spiritual part. The dream that death is an emancipation of the spiritual essence from a body that imprisons and clogs it, and is in itself the entrance on a freer, larger life, belongs to the schools, not to Christianity. The

[1] The subject is more fully treated by the present writer in his *Christian View of God and the World*, Lect. V., with Appendix, and *God's Image in Man*, Lect. VI.

disembodied state is never presented in Scripture
—Old Testament or New—as other than one of
incomplete being—of enfeebled life, diminished
powers, restricted capacities of action. " Sheol,"
" Hades," is not the abode of true immortality.
It follows that salvation from a state of sin which
has brought man under the law of death must
include deliverance from this incomplete condition. It must include deliverance from Sheol—
" the redemption of the body." The Redeemer
must be One who holds " the keys of death and of
Hades."[1] It must embrace resurrection.

In a previous chapter it was hinted that this is
probably the proper direction in which to look
for the origin of the Biblical idea of resurrection,
and of the form which the hope of immortality
assumed in the Old Testament. The believing
relation to God is felt to carry in it the pledge of
deliverance even from Sheol, and of a restored and
perfected life in God's presence. It is significant
that Jesus quotes the declaration, " I am the God
of Abraham, and the God of Isaac, and the God
of Jacob "[2] in proof, not simply of the continued
subsistence of the patriarchs in some state of being,
but of the resurrection of the dead. The late
Dr. A. B. Davidson unexceptionably states the
point in the following words of his *Commentary on
Job*. " The human spirit," he says, " is conscious

[1] Rev. i. 18.   [2] Matt. xxii. 23.

of fellowship with God, and this fellowship, from the nature of God, is a thing imperishable, and, in spite of obscurations, it must yet be fully manifested by God. This principle, grasped with convulsive earnestness in the prospect of death, became the Hebrew doctrine of immortality. This doctrine was but the necessary corollary of religion. In this life the true relations of men to God were felt to be realized ; and the Hebrew faith of immortality— never a belief in the mere existence of the soul after death, for the lowest superstition assumed this—was a faith that the dark and mysterious event of death would not interrupt the life of the person with God, enjoyed in this world. . . . The doctrine of immortality in the book [of Job] is the same as that of other parts of the Old Testament. Immortality is the corollary of religion. If there be religion—that is, if God be—there is immortality, not of the soul, but of the whole personal being of man (Ps. xvi. 9). This teaching of the whole Old Testament is expressed by our Lord with a surprising incisiveness in two sentences, ' I am the *God* of Abraham, God is not the God of the dead but the God of the *living.*' " [1]

How essential the Resurrection of Jesus is as an integral part of a doctrine of Redemption will appear from such considerations without further comment.

[1] *Com. on Job,* Appendix, pp. 293-5.

(3) A last aspect, intimately connected with the foregoing, in which the doctrinal significance of the Resurrection is perceived, is in its relation to the *believer's own hope* of resurrection. This is the point of view from which the Resurrection is treated in that great pæan of resurrection hope— the fifteenth chapter of I Corinthians. Christ's Resurrection is the ground and pledge of the resurrection of believers. If Christ has not risen, neither can they rise. The Christian dead have perished.[1] So completely does St. Paul bind up survival after death with the hope of resurrection that, in the denial of the latter, he apparently feels the ground to be taken from the former as well. Immortality, with him, for the Christian, is " incorruption "[2]— victory over death in body as in soul. In Christ's Resurrection, the assurance of that victory is given. " But now hath Christ been raised, the first fruits of them that are asleep . . . Christ the firstfruits : then they that are Christ's, at His coming."[3] This sheds again a broad, clear light on the nature of the Christian's hope of immortality. It is no mere futurity of existence—no mere ghostly persistence after death. It is an immortality of positive life, of holiness, of blessedness, of glory—of perfected likeness to Christ in body, soul and spirit.[4] It is here that the thought of resurrection

---

[1] I Cor. xv. 18.   [2] I Cor. xv. 42, 52–4 ; 2 Tim. i. 10.
[3] Cor. xv. 20, 23.   [4] Phil. iii. 20–21 ; cf. I John iii. 2.

helps, for once more the Redemption of Christ is seen to be a redemption of the whole man—body and soul together.

The difficulties which present themselves on the subject of the resurrection of the body are, of course, manifold, and cannot be ignored. The difficulty is greater even than in the case of Jesus, for there Resurrection took place within three days, in a body which had not seen corruption. But the bodies of the generations of the Christian dead have utterly perished. How is resurrection possible for them ? The Apostle does indeed speak of the bodies of those who are alive at the Parousia being "changed." [1] But this obviously leaves untouched the case of the vast majority who have died "in faith" in the interval.

The subject is full of mystery. The error lies in conceiving of the resurrection of the body of the Christian as necessarily the raising again of the very material form that was deposited in the grave. This, though the notion has been defended, loads the doctrine of the resurrection with a needless weight and is not required by anything contained in Scripture. St. Paul, indeed, using the analogy of the seed-corn, says expressly : "Thou sowest not the body that shall be. . . . But God giveth it a body as it pleased Him." [2] There is here iden-

---

[1] I Cor. xv. 51–2 ; I Thess. iv. 15–18.
[2] I Cor. xv. 37–8.

tity between the old self and the new even as regards the body.   But it is not identity of the same
material substance.   In truth, as has often been
pointed out, the identity of our bodies, even on
earth, does not consist in sameness of material
particles.   The matter in our bodies is continually
changing : in the course of a few years has entirely
changed.   The bond of identity is in something
deeper, in the abiding organizing principle which
serves as the thread of connexion amidst all changes.
That endures, is not allowed to be destroyed at
death ; and stamps its individuality and all it in-
herits from the old body upon the new.

Questions innumerable doubtless may be asked
which it is not possible to answer.   How, for example, can a body so transformed as to be called
" spiritual " yet retain the true character of a
" body " ?   What place is there for " body " in
a spiritual realm at all ?   No place, assuredly, for
the body of " flesh " ($\sigma \acute{\alpha} \rho \xi$) ; but for a body ($\sigma \hat{\omega} \mu \alpha$)
of another kind, there not only may be, but, if Jesus
has passed into the heavens, there *is*, place.   " There
are also," the Apostle says, " celestial bodies, and
bodies terrestrial." [1]   Such a body, adapted to
celestial conditions, will be the resurrection body of
the believer.   Even already a hidden tie connects

[1] I Cor. xv. 40.   The remarks on this subject in Stewart
and Tait's book, *The Unseen Universe*, are worth consulting as coming from men of scientific eminence.   Cf. pp.
26–7, but specially pp. 157–163.

this future resurrection-body with the Resurrection life of the Redeemer. For the production of this body the possession of the Spirit of the Risen Lord is necessary. On the other hand, where that Spirit is present, the forces for the production of the resurrection-body are at work—conceivably the basis of it is being already laid within the body that now is. Hardly less seems to be the meaning of the Apostle's words: " If Christ be in you, the body is dead because of sin ; but the Spirit is life because of righteousness. But if the Spirit of Him that raised up Jesus from the dead dwell in you, He that raised up Christ Jesus from the dead shall quicken also your mortal bodies through His Spirit that dwelleth in you." [1]

In conclusion, the Resurrection of Jesus stands fast as a fact, unaffected by the boastful waves of scepticism that ceaselessly through the ages beat themselves against it ; retains its significance as a corner-stone in the edifice of human redemption ; and holds within it the vastest hope for time and for eternity that humanity can ever know.

" Blessed be the God and Father of our Lord Jesus Christ, who, according to His great mercy, begat us again unto a living hope, by the Resurrection of Jesus Christ from the dead, unto an inheritance incorruptible, undefiled, and that fadeth not away." [2]

---

[1] Rom. viii. 10, 11.   [2] 1 Pet. i. 3, 4.

INDEX

Abbott, E. A., 64, 66
Alford, Dean, 59, 65 ff., 123,
    152, 160, 166, 179, 185
Allen, W. C., 18, 20, 61,
    124, 190, 191
Apocryphal beliefs, 170, 259
    ff.
Apparitional theory, 27, 226
    ff. (*See* Resurrection.)
Arnold, T., 10.
Ascension of Christ, 152,
    156, 192 ff.

Balfour, A. J., 17
Baur, F., 38, 68
Beyschlag, W., 225, 231
Boissier, G., 237
Bousset, W., 16, 44, 267
Bruce, A. B., 51, 220–1
Burkitt, F. C., 34, 59, 61 ff.,
    67 ff., 72, 73, 95
Bushnell, H., 52
Butler, Bishop, 51–2

Campbell, Dr. Colin, 69
Campbell, R. J., 91, 201
Celsus, 10, 20
Cheyne, T. K., 21–3, 116,
    236, 238–9, 248–50, 254,
    258

Ebrard, 166

Farnell, L. H., 21, 236
Frazer, J. G., 21
Forrest, D. W., 54, 160
Foster, G. B., 16, 49

Butler and Tanner, The Selwood Printing Works, Frome, and London

CPSIA information can be obtained
at www.ICGtesting.com
Printed in the USA
LVOW07s1625260617
539414LV00012B/923/P